Developing Communications Skills for the Accounting Profession

WITHDRAWN

Developing Communications Skills for the Accounting Profession

by
Robert W. Ingram
(Division of Accounting)
and
Charles R. Frazier
(English Department)
University of South Carolina

American Accounting Association

Copyright, American Accounting Association, 1980, All rights reserved
Library of Congress Catalog Card Number 80-52474
ISBN 0-86539-035-5
Printed in the United States of America

American Accounting Association
5717 Bessie Drive
Sarasota, Florida 33583

254172

HF
5657
I55

Contents

Foreword

A common complaint of both professors and practitioners is that accounting students and recent graduates cannot speak and write effectively. Indeed, this inability to communicate is often cited as the greatest single deficiency in junior staff accountants. Most of these complaints are merely anecdotal, however. The unique contribution of this research study is that it identifies the views of both faculty members and practitioners regarding the communications skills that students and staff accountants need and the extent to which they actually demonstrate those skills. Thus, it injects a note of scientific inquiry into discussions too often marked by innuendo and invective.

The research project described in this volume was commissioned by Leon E. Hay, my predecessor as Director of Education. It is a pleasure for me to make it available to all who are concerned about a very real problem. It is to be hoped that Professors Ingram and Frazier's findings and recommendations will help lead the way to a solution to that problem.

James M. Fremgen
Director of Education
1979-80

Acknowledgments

A number of individuals contributed significantly to this study. The project was commissioned while Leon E. Hay was Director of Education of the American Accounting Association. Professor Hay was instrumental in the developmental stages of the project. The Advisory Committee consisted of:

Roger Eickhoff, Touche Ross & Company
Jay M. Smith, Brigham Young University
Jan R. Williams, University of Tennessee (Chairman)

The Committee provided valuable assistance throughout the project from proposal to final draft. Committee members' suggestions were helpful in developing questionnaires and in preparing drafts of the manuscript. Their careful attention to the project and patience in its progress are greatly appreciated. Also, considerable assistance was provided by James M. Fremgen, the current Director of Education for the Association. Professor Fremgen was very helpful in reviewing the manuscript. While all of these individuals made contributions to the study, any remaining errors are the sole responsibility of the authors.

One

Introduction

Communications skills are a very important requirement for success in the accounting profession. It is not uncommon to hear practitioners discuss the role of effective communications in the everyday activities of accountants and stress the need for development of these skills in entry-level personnel. Most accounting educators are exposed to student communications problems and are known frequently to lament the deficiencies evident in these skills. The need apparently exists within the accounting profession for the development of communications skills. Unfortunately, however, little direct attention appears to have been focused on this problem by academicians.

Objectives

The present study is offered as a preliminary investigation of the nature and magnitude of the problem. The study attempts to bring attention to the problem of developing communications skills, to arouse interest in the subject among academicians and practitioners, and to provide an introduction to the topic for those who might become interested in examining the relationship between accounting and communications. The objectives of the study are (1) to assess the types of communications skills which practitioners and academicians perceive to be needed by entry-level accountants and to identify perceived deficiencies in these skills, (2) to examine the effect which deficiencies in these skills have on the behavior of CPA firms and industries which employ accountants, particularly in terms of hiring and dismissal practices, (3) to examine efforts currently being made by accounting programs to develop communications skills, and (4) to delineate alternatives which accounting faculties can consider in attempting to address the needs identified in the study.

Definitions

As used in this research, the term "communications skills" refers to both oral and written processes and incorporates such basic elements as organization, grammar, syntax, and rhetoric. Business communications normally include such topics as report writing and presentation, research, memorandums, interviews, and small group interaction. The study is limited to skills needed and displayed by entry-level personnel since graduates of accounting programs normally fit this category and since academicians are presumed, therefore, to be particularly interested in the qualifications of these individuals. For simplicity, the term "staff accountant" is used throughout this report to refer to these subjects. Staff accountants are defined for our purposes as junior level accounting personnel, in the first three years of employment, whose duties require active involvement in communications processes. Personnel involved in purely clerical or managerial duties are exempted from consideration. This definition is somewhat arbitrary but delimits the study to a reasonable set of subjects who are products of the accounting education process.

Organization

The remaining chapters of this report describe the methodology used to achieve the objectives set forth above and discuss the results of the research as they pertain to each objective. Preliminary to these sections, it is important that the reader be aware of the body of literature on the subject of communications in accounting and business. The remainder of this chapter introduces this literature in order that the reader may place the current study in perspective, understand the background from which the methlology and analysis sections of this report are derived, and have a place to begin if further exploration of the subject is desired. The section is an introduction and not an exhaustive survey. The selected bibliography at the end of this report contains some of the more significant articles on the subject, and the reader is referred to these for additional information.

Literature Review

The body of literature on the topic of business communications is both extensive and diverse in approach and purpose. Rather than attempting to discuss the literature in general, it is perhaps more useful to categorize and indicate representative articles within each category. Most work in this field falls into one of the following categories: (1)

articles which attempt to give advice on basic writing skills, (2) articles which deal with aspects of the pedagogy of business communications, and (3) articles which are directly research oriented.

Much of the available published material on writing for the business world is in the form of practical advice on how to improve basic writing skills. These articles, published primarily in practice-oriented journals, typically suggest techniques for improving skills in writing memos, letters, and short reports. Many of them simply adapt to business writing the precepts of basic writing guides such as the Strunk and White [1959] classic, *The Elements of Style*. Typical of this type of article are those by Rice [1976], John [1976], Sigband [1976], Ley [1974], and Swift [1973]. Each of these articles stresses the need for clarity, brevity, directness, and accuracy in written communications. In addition, most of these articles suggest useful patterns of organization and advice on such matters as diction choice, use of the active voice, and layout. In a similar, though more thorough and specific article, Locker [1977] discusses methods of organization for business communications and emphasizes the need for persuasive techniques and psychological rather than logical patterns of organization. In an article which runs counter to the notion to strict adherence to short, simple sentences that many business writers and writing teachers advocate, Foley [1974] argues that effective, clear communication results from adapting sentence length and structure to the relative complexity of the idea being communicated.

Articles on business communications pedagogy range in topic from explanations of effective teaching techniques to discussions of the ideological underpinnings of writing courses and programs. Representative of the former type is Baker and Ashby's "Teaching Business Writing by the Spiral Method" [1977] which discusses methods of teaching the steps in the process of prewriting, writing, and rewriting. Swenson [1973] suggests simulation, role playing, and group presentations as effective techniques for the business communications classroom. Hall argues that learning a "psychological approach to both oral and written expression" is an important objective for the student in a business communications course. Among those treating broader aspects of business communications courses is Sullivan [1977], who examines the philosophical foundations of several approaches to the teaching of such classes. Sullivan concludes that his perception of the present healthy mixture of philosophies is threatened by the increasing dominance of scientific realism-behaviorism.

Of the research oriented articles, most involve surveys concerning various aspects of business communications. Huegli and Tschirgi [1974] surveyed recent business graduates on the communications skills required by their jobs and their degree of proficiency in performing those skills. Supervisors were also interviewed concerning the communications effectiveness of these new employees. Based on the data obtained, Huegli and Tschirgi pointed out a significant discrepancy between the entry-level employees' perceptions of their communications skills and the evaluation of their performance by the supervisors. Most of the supervisors indicated that entry-level employees lacked adequate proficiency in the communications requirements of their jobs. Huegli and Tschirgi also noted that, though employees report using oral communications skills far more frequently than written skills, their responses show a desire for improved letter and reporting writing, an inconsistency which may indicate that "new employees avoid using written media when they can because they are not effective in using it."

Rainey [1972] surveyed AACSB professors and corporate executives and found agreement between the two groups on the desirability of courses in business report writing and advanced courses in business communications. The executives surveyed considered the ability to write "routine" letters, "persuasive" letters, and "routine" reports to be the most important writing skills for an employee. Also, the executives attached more importance to proposal writing and to courses devoted to analyzing letters, reports, and proposals than did the professors.

Penrose [1976] sent questionnaires concerning the importance of twelve business-related skills to a sample of local businessmen. Skills in business speaking and business writing ranked fifth and sixth behind public relations, marketing, accounting, and finance. Penrose suggests this "somewhat unexpected weak showing" might be improved significantly by combining writing and speaking skills as "Business Communications."

Andrews and Koester [1979] surveyed recently graduated accountants and their employers, including CPA firms, corporations, and government agencies. Questionnaires also were sent to accounting educators and senior accounting majors. The questions were designed to distinguish between problems in written and oral communication. Responses to the questions indicated that respondents in all categories are less satisfied with the recent graduates' writing skills than with their oral skills. Similarly, when asked what form of communication seemed most difficult for the employee, respondents ranked nonnumerical report writing significantly higher than oral presentation. However, when asked in which areas students need more training, respondents placed considerably more emphasis on oral communication than on other areas. Andrews and Koester argue that a reason for this inconsistency may be that "accounting professionals, while concerned about writing skills, feel that the proposed areas of training are inadequate; and these professionals also feel that oral presentation skills are, more properly, the province of the academic classroom while training in writing can be done in-house."

Stine and Skarzenski [1979] sent questionnaires to businessmen and academicians. The survey concentrated on the kinds of communications skills needed by business and the relative importance of these skills. Executives indicated clarity, brevity, organization, and the mechanics of grammar and spelling as the most valued writing skills, and they pointed to letters, memos, and short reports as the most important forms of writing. Faculty members generally agreed with the executives on writing skills, but they tended to emphasize more extended forms of writing such as technical reports and long reports. Both the executives and faculty claimed they expect white-collar workers to spend 75 to 80 percent of their on-the-job time in written and oral communication.

The present study fits into the third category and extends previous research into the needs and deficiencies of communications skills in the accounting profession. This research differs from previous studies in that it (1) concentrates on the accounting profession specifically, (2) examines the need for and demonstrated ability of specific communications skills, (3) examines the potential consequences of deficiencies and the impact on firms' behavior, (4) assesses the nature and extent of current efforts by academicians to develop communications skills in accounting programs, and (5) explores possible modifications of the accounting curriculum which might improve the development of these skills. Thus, the current study is a more extensive examination of the communications skills problems of the accounting profession than previously has been undertaken.

Two

Methodology

The research methodology used in this study is based on an opinion survey of practicing accountants and academicians. Mail questionnaires were used to elicit responses concerning a variety of topics involving the importance of specific communications skills and the effect that consideration of these skills has on professional and academic activities.

Sample

Questionnaires were sent to practicing accountants selected from CPA firms and private industries and to academicians in domestic colleges and universities. A sample of public practitioners was derived from a list of the 103 largest CPA firms as provided by the AICPA and from *Accounting Firms and Practitioners* [AICPA, 1977]. A questionnaire was mailed to the personnel director of each of the 103 largest firms and to the personnel directors of 52 randomly selected firms from the AICPA publication. The sample size was judgmentally selected to be representative of the population of CPA firms but weighted towards larger firms which hire the largest percentage of accounting graduates. *A priori,* firms which are actively involved in the job market are in a better position to evaluate skills displayed and needed by recent graduates.

A sample of corporations was selected from Fortune 500 firms. A questionnaire was mailed to the controller of each of 155 randomly selected firms. [1] Again, the sample size was judgmentally selected to be representative of the population of larger firms which are likely to be involved in the market for accounting graduates.

---

[1] Questionnaires were mailed to controllers in industrial firms rather than personnel directors since personnel directors in industry are involved with numerous employees who are not accountants. Accordingly, they may have had more difficulty in restricting their responses to include only accounting communications than would individuals in charge of the accounting function or an assistant in the controller's department who works directly with accounting personnel.

The letters which accompanied these questionnaires (see Appendix A) requested that the questionnaires be completed by the recipient or by someone else in the organization who is involved in the supervision of accounting personnel. This procedure was used to reduce the probability that the questionnaire would be disregarded because the recipient was not in a position to evaluate employee communications skills and firm practices and to minimize the number of poorly qualified respondents.

A third sample of respondents was selected by mailing questionnaires to the department administrators of the 259 domestic colleges and universities listed as offering accounting programs in Hasselback [1977]. The letter accompanying these questionnaires (Appendix B) also requested that the questionnaire be completed by the recipient or someone on the faculty who was in a position to evaluate student communications skills and skills development in the accounting program.

All of the letters requested that the questionnaires be returned regardless of whether they were completed. This procedure was used to ensure that the questionnaires had been received and to determine whether a second mailing would be useful. A second mailing was sent to accounting practitioners who had responded within three weeks of the first mailing. A second mailing was not considered necessary for the academic group because of the response rate for the first mailing.

The number of responses to each of these mailings is shown in Table 1. Two mailings were needed to secure an adequate response rate from accounting practitioners. While nearly 40 percent of the questionnaires from the first mailing were returned, a number of these were not completed. Approximately two-thirds of the practitioner firms returned one of the two mailings and a larger than 40 percent usable response rate was secured. A similar response rate was obtained from one mailing to academicians, and a second mailing was not considered necessary. The number of responses was well distributed across response groups with approximately a 40 percent usable response rate from each group (see Table 1).

Academic responses were further divided according to the highest degree offered by the respondent's university as shown in Table 1. This division is useful for assessing the representativeness of the respondents. It may also be useful for determining whether attitudes about communications skills vary systematically according to the type of academic programs offered by a university.

TABLE 1

Respondents	Sample Size	Responses* Mailing 1	Mailing 2	Usable Responses	Usable Response Rate (Percent)
Practitioners:					
CPA firms					
Largest 103	103	35	33	44	42.7
Other	52	21	11	20	38.5
Subtotal	155	56	44	64	41.3
Fortune 500	155	62	47	70	45.2
Total Practitioners	310	118	91	134	43.2
Academicians:					
Highest Degree Offered					
Bachelor's		37	—	35	
Master's		54	—	51	
Doctorate		30	—	28	
Total Academicians	259	121	—	114	44.0

*Includes completed and uncompleted questionnaires.

Questionnaire Design

Two questionnaires were used in the study (Appendices C and D). One was sent to the sample of practitioners and the other was sent to the sample of academicians. Both questionnaires contained a "communications skills inventory." The inventory consisted of 20 skills which are potentially useful to staff accountants. The skills were divided into four groups: forms of communication, mechanical skills, logic and organization skills, and stylistic skills. These groups were selected after an extensive review of the communications literature to identify types of skills which might be useful to staff accountants. The list of skills is not intended to be exhaustive but rather to be representative of the range and types of skills needed by accountants. An attempt was also made to separate the list into individual skills so that respondents could identify clearly which specific activity they were considering. A list of definitions was provided with the questionnaires (Appendix E) to reduce differences in interpretation of items across respondents.

All respondents were asked to indicate their opinions of the extent to which each of the skills in the inventory was needed by staff accounting personnel. Respondents were asked to respond to the following statement for each skill: This is a skill frequently necessary for the successful completion of staff accountant responsibilities. Opinions were indicated from a six-point scale: (1) strongly disagree, (2) disagree, (3) neutral, (4) agree, (5) strongly agree, and (6) can't evaluate.

In addition, accounting practitioners were requested to express an opinion concerning the extent to which staff accountants successfully demonstrate each of the inventory skills. They responded to the statement: This is a skill successfully demonstrated by most staff accountants. The same six-point scale was used as the one used for assessing necessary skills. Academicians were also requested to respond to the statement but the words "accounting graduates" were substituted for "staff accountants."

The two sets of responses for necessary and demonstrated skills for each class of respondent permitted analysis of the importance of each skill and of the preparation received by accounting graduates in each skill. Differences in opinion could also be assessed among groups of respondents. This analysis should provide assistance in determining where additional emphasis should be placed in developing communications skills and whether there is general agreement concerning this emphasis.

The remainder of the questionnaire mailed to practitioners sought information concerning the perceived impact of communications skills on a firm's behavior in terms of hiring and dismissal practices and in terms of firms' efforts to improve employee communications skills. Practitioners were asked how frequently the lack of communications skills was (1) a primary or (2) a contributing reason for not hiring or for dismissing an individual. Responses were selected from the following scale: (1) very frequently, (2) frequently, (3) sometimes, (4) not often, (5) never, and (6) can't evaluate. Practitioners were also requested to identify the specific skills which contributed most frequently to decisions not to hire or to dismiss an individual.

These questions should be useful for evaluating the possible effect which communications skills deficiencies can have on accounting graduates and whether dissatisfaction on the part of practitioners with these skills may result in behavioral as well as attitudinal responses. These questions are also useful for validating the responses to the skills inventory.

In addition to the skills inventory, the questionnaire mailed to academicians requested information concerning course offerings and other efforts of accounting programs to develop communications skills. Respondents were requested to indicate whether communications courses (other than general education requirements) were available to accounting students at the undergraduate or graduate level. Information was sought concerning whether these courses were recommended or required; were taught by accounting, business or nonbusiness faculty; and were offered with credit. If courses were not available to accounting students, respondents were asked to indicate the reason. A list of potential responses was provided.

Since specialized courses are only one method for developing communications skills, academicians were asked to indicate the approximate percentage of instructional hours devoted to communications skills at the undergraduate and graduate levels. This question permits analysis of whether the major efforts to develop skills are confined to specific course offerings or whether significant efforts are being made to develop skills by incorporating these activities into other aspects of the curriculum.

Academicians were asked to indicate their opinions of the quality of communications skills displayed by their accounting graduates. Respondents were also requested to indicate their perceptions of changes in the emphasis placed on communications skills in their programs. These questions are useful for validating responses to the skills inventory and for assessing the probability that awareness of communications skills deficiencies is leading to modification of accounting programs.

Finally, academicians were asked to indicate the degree programs (undergraduate, master's, doctorate) offered to accounting majors. Responses to this question were used to group respondents according to the highest degree offered.

Reliability and Validity

Reliability and validity are important attributes of attitude research (see Grove and Savich [1979]). Several steps were taken in this study to maximize the probability that the results of the survey would measure what they were intended to measure and that the results were representative of the populations from which they were drawn.

Throughout the questionnaire design phase, the advisory committee played an active role in reviewing and recommending modifications of the questionnaires. The questionnaires were pretested by both practicing accountants and academicians and modifications were made to improve understandability and response validity. A set of definitions was provided along with the questionnaires to increase uniformity in understanding of specific items.

The number of responses from each group of respondents was checked to ensure adequate representation from each group. Nonresponse bias was also assessed. The procedures used for this purpose assumed that late respondents were similar to nonrespondents and late responses were compared to early responses to determine the presence of bias (see Oppenheim [1966]). The practitioner responses were assessed by comparing responses to the first mailing with responses to the second mailing. Academic responses were assessed by comparing responses to questionnaires received within the three weeks after the mailing (76 percent) to those received after this period. Correlations across individual items in these sets of questionnaires revealed no substantive differences.

Only questionnaires which were fully completed were used in the analysis and internal validity was evaluated in these questionnaires by comparing responses to the skills inventory with questions concerning hiring and dismissal practices in practitioner responses. A more general assessment of internal validity was made in academic responses by comparing responses to the skills inventory with questions concerning the perceived proficiency of accounting graduates. These comparisons revealed no evidence which would suggest the respondents were not consistent in their answers.

Analysis of Responses

Since the level of measurement used in this study was not greater than the nominal or ordinal scale, nonparametric tests of differences among groups were employed. Medians are provided as the primary measure of central tendency with means and standard deviations provided for comparison.

Analysis of responses focused on identifying specific skills and groups of skills which were perceived by respondents to be most necessary for successful completion of staff accountant duties. Perceptions of deficiencies in these skills were also examined, and comparisons were made to determine differences in the perceptions between CPAs and industrial accountants and among academicians grouped by the highest degree offered in their respective programs. Differences between the perceptions of practitioners and academicians were also examined. Chi-square tests were used in these analyses.

These analyses were used to determine whether the perceptions of public practitioners differ from their industrial counterparts as to the skills needed and displayed by staff accountants. A lack of consensus between these groups would suggest that different skills were needed by accountants in these different positions and would suggest where additional emphasis should be placed in developing required skills. Differences among the perceptions of groups of academicians might indicate perceptual bias or different orientations within these groups.

Differences between perceptions of academicians and those of practitioners might suggest the need for modification of academic curricula to serve better the needs of the profession or to address deficiencies in current programs.

Descriptive statistics (median, mean, frequency) provide the basis for much of the remaining analysis. These statistics were used to identify needed and displayed skills, deficiencies which affect hiring and dismissal practices of practitioners, and the nature of course offerings and emphases in academic program. Results of these analyses are provided in the following sections.

Three

Perceptions of Communications Skills Needed and Displayed by Recent Accounting Graduates

One of the primary objectives of this study is to identify the types of communications skills needed by staff accountants and to identify deficiencies in these skills. This information should be useful for designing or modifying accounting curricula to prepare accounting graduates better for careers in the profession.

Practitioners' Perceptions of Needed Skills

Results of the communications skills inventory are shown in Table 2. This table indicates the percentage response for each point on the scale used for public practitioner and industrial groups and for the total sample. The median, mean, and standard deviation are also shown for each group and the combined sample. "Can't evaluate" responses were excluded from these computations since they are not part of the ordinal scale used in the remaining responses.

Median and mean statistics are very similar across all skills and standard deviations averaged about .6 for most items, suggesting a large degree of consensus across respondents. The large majority of respondents indicated a neutral, agree, or strongly agree response to the statement that the skills were needed for all of the skills in the inventory. Only "the use of visual aids" item received a number of disagree responses. Medians for all of the items were above 4.0 (indicating clear agreement) for the total sample except for reading speed, formal oral presentation, and use of visual aids. Of the remaining skills listed, a number received similar scores and no attempt has been made to rank these. Instead, it appears that practitioners clearly agree that communications skills are necessary for the successful completion of staff accountant duties. Of the represented skills, the mechanical and organization groups were all rated very highly, and nearly all of the skills in the forms of communications and stylistic skills groups received high ratings.

Although little disagreement between the CPA group and industrial group was evident for most skills, a few differences were detected. All of the skills except listening attentiveness, outline development, and use of visual aids received higher scores from the CPA group, suggesting that this group perceives, on average, communications skills to be more important. This phenomenon is logical since employees of CPA firms (especially at the staff level) are likely to have more public contact than those of industrial firms.

These differences can also be observed for those skills in which the differences between the two groups are significant (as measured by the Chi-Square tests). These differences were observed for correspondence writing, formal report writing, reading speed, listening responsiveness, correct grammar, correct punctuation, correct spelling, and paragraph development. All of these skills received significantly higher ratings (at $\alpha = .10$) from the CPA group. These differences, however, do not detract from the overall indication that both groups perceived nearly all of the listed skills and groups of skills to be important for staff accountants.

Practitioners' Perceptions of Demonstrated Skills

A similar analysis to the above was made for each of the skills in the inventory to assess whether respondents agreed that staff accountants adequately demonstrate these skills. Results of this analysis are indicated in Table 3. Again, median and mean responses are similar for each item, although the standard deviations are larger than those in Table 2.

Scores for all skill items were lower than in the previous analysis. For the total sample, scores ranged from a low of 2.23 for formal report writing to a high of 3.62 for listening attentiveness. Ten of the skills received a mean rating of less than 3, indicating an overall disagreement with the statement that the skill was adequately demon-

PRACTITIONERS' PERCEPTIONS OF COMMUNICATIONS SKILLS NEEDED BY STAFF ACCOUNTANTS

Skill	Group	Strongly Disagree (1)	Disagree (2)	Neutral (3)	Agree (4)	Strongly Agree (5)	Can't Evaluate	Median (1-5)	Mean (1-5)	SD (1-5)
Correspondence Writing	CPA	1.5%	1.5%	6.1%	37.9%	48.5%	1.5%	4.48	4.29	.897
	IND	1.3	7.6	13.9	51.9	25.3	0	4.02	3.92	.903
	TOTAL	1.4	6.2	10.3	45.5	35.9	.7	4.20	4.09	.915
	[Chi-Square 10.8, Significance .055]									
Memorandums and Informal Report Writing	CPA	0	0	2.5	33.3	62.1	1.5	4.71	4.60	.553
	IND	0	1.3	3.0	44.3	51.9	0	4.54	4.47	.617
	TOTAL	0	.7	2.8	39.3	56.6	.7	4.62	4.53	.591
	[Chi-Square 3.8, Significance .430]									
Formal Report Writing	CPA	0	3.0	12.1	36.4	45.5	3.0	4.42	4.28	.806
	IND	1.3	8.9	25.3	35.4	29.1	0	3.91	3.82	.997
	TOTAL	.7	6.2	19.3	35.9	36.6	1.4	4.14	4.03	.942
	[Chi-Square 11.1, Significance .050]									
Reading Speed	CPA	1.5	6.1	21.2	42.4	27.3	1.5	3.98	3.89	.937
	IND	0	11.4	26.6	51.9	10.1	0	3.73	3.61	.823
	TOTAL	.7	9.0	24.1	47.6	17.9	.7	3.83	3.74	.885
	[Chi-Square 10.5, Significance .061]									
Reading Comprehension	CPA	0	0	0	34.8	63.6	1.5	4.73	4.65	.482
	IND	0	0	2.5	38.0	59.5	0	4.66	4.57	.547
	TOTAL	0	0	1.4	36.6	61.4	.7	4.69	4.60	.518
	[Chi-Square 3.1, Significance .382]									
Informal Oral Presentation	CPA	0	0	7.6	34.8	54.5	3.0	4.61	4.48	.642
	IND	0	1.3	7.6	50.6	39.2	1.3	4.30	4.30	.667
	TOTAL	0	.7	7.6	43.4	46.2	2.1	4.44	4.38	.660
	[Chi-Square 5.3, Significance .262]									

TABLE 2 (Continued)

Skill	Group	Strongly Disagree (1)	Disagree (2)	Neutral (3)	Agree (4)	Strongly Agree (5)	Can't Evaluate	Median (1-5)	Mean (1-5)	SD (1-5)
Formal Oral Presentation	CPA	1.5%	12.1%	16.7%	45.5%	21.2%	3.0%	3.90	3.75	.992
	IND	5.1	15.2	30.4	35.4	13.9	0	3.48	3.38	1.066
	TOTAL	3.4	12.1	24.1	40.0	17.2	1.4	3.70	3.55	1.046
	[Chi-Square 8.8, Significance .119]									
Listening Attentiveness	CPA	0	0	0	25.8	72.7	1.5	4.72	4.74	.443
	IND	0	0	3.8	38.0	57.0	1.3	4.63	4.54	.574
	TOTAL	0	0	2.1	32.4	64.1	1.4	4.73	4.63	.526
	[Chi-Square 5.6, Significance .134]									
Listening Responsiveness	CPA	0	0	1.5	30.3	63.6	4.5	4.75	4.65	.513
	IND	0	0	6.3	46.8	44.3	2.5	4.41	4.39	.610
	TOTAL	0	0	4.1	39.3	53.1	3.4	4.59	4.51	.581
	[Chi-Square 7.5, Significance .058]									
Correct Grammar	CPA	0	0	0	22.7	75.8	1.5	4.85	4.77	.425
	IND	0	1.3	3.8	46.8	48.1	0	4.46	4.42	.633
	TOTAL	0	.7	2.1	35.9	60.7	.7	4.68	4.58	.574
	[Chi-Square 14.9, Significance .005]									
Correct Punctuation	CPA	0	0	7.6	30.3	60.6	1.5	4.69	4.54	.639
	IND	0	1.3	10.1	53.2	35.4	0	4.23	4.23	.678
	TOTAL	0	.7	9.0	42.8	46.9	.7	4.44	4.37	.677
	[Chi-Square 11.5, Significance .021]									
Correct Spelling	CPA	0	1.5	3.0	21.2	72.7	1.5	4.82	4.68	.615
	IND	0	1.3	6.3	51.9	40.5	0	4.32	4.32	.651
	TOTAL	0	1.4	4.8	37.9	55.2	.7	4.60	4.48	.658
	[Chi-Square 17.7, Significance .001]									

TABLE 2 (Continued)

Skill	Group	Strongly Disagree (1)	Disagree (2)	Neutral (3)	Agree (4)	Strongly Agree (5)	Can't Evaluate	Median (1-5)	Mean (1-5)	SD (1-5)
Outline Development	CPA	0%	0%	7.6%	51.5%	39.4%	1.5%	4.31	4.32	.615
	IND	0	1.3	6.3	45.6	45.6	1.3	4.42	4.37	.667
	TOTAL	0	.7	6.9	48.3	42.8	1.4	4.36	4.35	.642
	[Chi-Square 1.5, Significance .824]									
Inductive Reasoning	CPA	0	0	4.5	40.9	51.5	3.0	4.60	4.54	.591
	IND	0	1.3	6.3	40.5	50.6	1.3	4.53	4.42	.675
	TOTAL	0	.7	5.5	40.7	51.0	2.1	4.54	4.45	.637
	[Chi-Square 1.6, Significance .810]									
Deductive Reasoning	CPA	0	0	3.0	36.4	57.6	3.0	4.66	4.56	.560
	IND	0	1.3	5.1	43.0	49.4	1.3	4.50	4.42	.655
	TOTAL	0	.7	4.1	40.0	53.1	2.1	4.58	4.49	.616
	[Chi-Square 2.6, Significance .628]									
Coherence in Verbal Presentation	CPA	0	0	0	48.5	50.0	1.5	4.52	4.50	.504
	IND	0	0	1.3	51.3	47.4	0	4.45	4.46	.527
	TOTAL	0	0	.7	50.0	48.6	.7	4.48	4.48	.515
	[Chi-Square 2.1, Significance .545]									
Clarity in Verbal Presentation	CPA	0	0	1.5	40.9	56.1	1.5	4.62	4.55	.531
	IND	0	1.3	2.5	51.9	44.3	0	4.39	4.39	.608
	TOTAL	0	.7	2.1	46.9	49.7	.7	4.50	4.47	.578
	[Chi-Square 4.1, Significance .388]									
Conciseness in Verbal Presentation	CPA	0	0	4.6	41.5	52.3	1.5	4.56	4.48	.591
	IND	0	0	5.1	55.7	39.2	0	4.31	4.34	.575
	TOTAL	0	0	4.9	49.3	45.1	.7	4.41	4.41	.584
	[Chi-Square 4.0, Significance .258]									

TABLE 2 (Continued)

Skill	Group	Strongly Disagree (1)	Disagree (2)	Neutral (3)	Agree (4)	Strongly Agree (5)	Can't Evaluate	Median (1-5)	Mean (1-5)	SD (1-5)
Paragraph Development	CPA	0%	3.0%	12.1%	50.0%	33.3%	1.5%	4.18	4.15	.755
	IND	0	1.3	11.4	72.2	13.9	1.3	4.01	4.00	.558
	TOTAL	0	2.1	11.7	62.1	22.8	1.4	4.07	4.07	.657
	[Chi-Square 9.4, Significance .053]									
Use of Visual Aids	CPA	6.1	13.6	41.8	27.3	6.1	4.5	3.16	3.14	.965
	IND	2.1	8.9	42.4	31.6	10.1	3.8	3.35	3.37	.936
	TOTAL	4.8	11.0	42.1	29.9	8.3	4.1	3.26	3.27	.952
	[Chi-Square 2.1, Significance .831]									

PRACTITIONERS' PERCEPTIONS OF COMMUNICATIONS SKILLS DEMONSTRATED BY STAFF ACCOUNTANTS

Skill	Group	Strongly Disagree (1)	Disagree (2)	Neutral (3)	Agree (4)	Strongly Agree (5)	Can't Evaluate	Median (1-5)	Mean (1-5)	SD (1-5)
Correspondence Writing	CPA	10.6%	51.5%	24.2%	13.6%	0%	0%	2.27	2.41	.859
	IND	10.4	33.8	28.6	22.1	1.3	3.9	2.64	2.69	.992
	TOTAL	10.5	42.0	26.6	18.2	.7	2.1	2.42	2.56	.939
	[Chi-Square 7.7, Significance .171]									
Memorandums and Informal Report Writing	CPA	6.1	39.4	34.8	19.7	0	0	2.63	2.68	.862
	IND	3.9	46.8	16.9	28.6	2.6	1.3	2.47	2.79	.998
	TOTAL	4.9	43.4	25.2	24.5	1.4	.7	2.56	2.74	.935
	[Chi-Square 9.1, Significance .107]									
Formal Report Writing	CPA	16.7	45.5	21.2	10.6	0	6.1	2.21	2.27	.890
	IND	11.7	45.5	20.8	16.9	0	5.2	2.29	2.45	.929
	TOTAL	14.0	45.5	21.0	14.0	0	5.6	2.23	2.37	.912
	[Chi-Square 1.7, Significance .794]									
Reading Speed	CPA	1.5	12.1	57.6	21.2	0	7.6	3.07	3.07	.655
	IND	.7	5.1	42.3	32.1	0	20.5	3.32	3.34	.599
	TOTAL	.7	8.3	49.3	27.1	0	14.6	3.18	3.20	.640
	[Chi-Square 10.6, Significance .031]									
Reading Comprehension	CPA	1.5	16.9	36.9	40.0	1.5	3.1	3.31	3.24	.817
	IND	.7	13.0	33.8	39.0	5.2	9.1	3.46	3.40	.806
	TOTAL	.7	14.8	35.2	39.4	3.5	6.3	3.39	3.22	.812
	[Chi-Square 5.0, Significance .414]									
Informal Oral Presentation	CPA	0	18.5	40.0	38.5	1.5	1.5	3.27	3.23	.771
	IND	0	19.5	33.5	42.9	1.3	2.6	3.37	3.27	.794
	TOTAL	0	19.0	36.6	40.8	1.4	2.1	3.32	3.25	.781
	[Chi-Square .7, Significance .944]									

TABLE 3 (Continued)

Skill	Group	Strongly Disagree (1)	Disagree (2)	Neutral (3)	Agree (4)	Strongly Agree (5)	Can't Evaluate	Median (1-5)	Mean (1-5)	SD (1-5)
Formal Oral Presentation	CPA	6.1%	37.9%	33.3%	16.7%	1.5%	4.5%	2.61	2.68	.895
	IND	3.9	28.6	41.6	13.0	0	13.0	2.77	2.73	.770
	TOTAL	4.9	32.9	37.8	14.7	.7	9.1	2.70	2.71	.830
	[Chi-Square 6.2, Significance .288]									
Listening Attentiveness	CPA	3.0	16.7	31.8	39.4	9.1	0	3.45	3.35	.969
	IND	0	7.9	28.9	53.9	6.6	2.6	3.72	3.61	.737
	TOTAL	1.4	12.0	30.3	47.2	7.7	1.4	3.62	3.49	.861
	[Chi-Square 8.3, Significance .142]									
Listening Responsiveness	CPA	1.5	21.2	33.3	37.9	4.5	1.5	3.30	3.23	.897
	IND	0	7.9	35.5	50.0	2.6	3.9	3.59	3.49	.690
	TOTAL	.7	14.1	34.5	44.4	3.5	2.8	3.48	3.37	.802
	[Chi-Square 7.9, Significance .160]									
Correct Grammar	CPA	3.0	47.0	22.7	25.8	1.5	0	2.50	2.76	.929
	IND	1.3	24.7	41.6	28.6	2.6	1.3	3.06	3.07	.838
	TOTAL	2.1	35.0	32.9	27.3	2.1	.7	2.88	2.92	.892
	[Chi-Square 10.6, Significance .061]									
Correct Punctuation	CPA	4.5	47.0	28.8	19.7	0	0	2.47	2.64	.853
	IND	2.6	31.2	37.7	26.0	1.3	1.3	2.91	2.92	.860
	TOTAL	3.5	38.5	33.6	23.1	.7	.7	2.73	2.79	.867
	[Chi-Square 5.8, Significance .321]									
Correct Spelling	CPA	7.6	34.8	31.8	24.2	1.5	0	2.74	2.77	.957
	IND	2.6	23.4	42.9	28.6	1.3	1.3	3.04	3.03	.832
	TOTAL	4.9	28.7	37.8	26.6	1.4	.7	2.93	2.91	.898
	[Chi Square 5.7, Significance .337]									

TABLE 3 (Continued)

Skill	Group	Strongly Disagree (1)	Disagree (2)	Neutral (3)	Agree (4)	Strongly Agree (5)	Can't Evaluate	Median (1-5)	Mean (1-5)	SD (1-5)
Outline Development	CPA	3.0%	30.3%	37.9%	25.8%	1.5%	1.5%	2.92	2.92	.872
	IND	1.3	22.7	34.7	36.0	0	5.3	3.17	3.11	.820
	TOTAL	2.1	26.2	36.2	31.2	.7	3.5	3.05	3.02	.847
[Chi-Square 5.1, Significance .402]										
Inductive Reasoning	CPA	1.5	21.5	36.9	38.5	1.5	0	3.23	3.17	.840
	IND	0	21.1	35.5	38.2	1.3	3.9	3.26	3.21	.799
	TOTAL	.7	21.3	36.2	38.3	1.4	2.1	3.25	3.19	.815
[Chi-Square 3.7, Significance .583]										
Deductive Reasoning	CPA	3.1	20.8	38.5	35.4	3.1	0	3.20	3.15	.888
	IND	0	15.8	42.1	36.8	1.3	3.9	3.27	3.25	.741
	TOTAL	1.4	17.7	40.4	36.2	2.1	2.1	3.24	3.20	.812
[Chi-Square 5.9, Significance .316]										
Coherence in Verbal Presentation	CPA	1.5	19.7	42.4	28.8	7.6	0	3.18	3.21	.903
	IND	2.6	14.3	39.0	39.0	2.6	2.6	3.32	3.25	.840
	TOTAL	2.1	16.8	40.6	34.3	4.9	1.4	3.25	3.23	.867
[Chi-Square 5.5, Significance .357]										
Clarity in Verbal Presentation	CPA	1.5	25.8	31.8	36.4	4.5	0	3.21	3.17	.921
	IND	2.6	18.2	44.2	32.5	1.3	1.3	3.15	3.12	.816
	TOTAL	2.1	21.7	38.5	34.3	2.8	.7	3.17	3.14	.864
[Chi-Square 4.9, Significance .428]										
Conciseness in Verbal Presentation	CPA	1.5	33.8	41.5	20.0	3.1	0	2.85	2.89	.850
	IND	3.9	24.7	48.1	20.8	1.3	1.2	2.93	2.91	.819
	TOTAL	2.8	28.9	45.1	20.4	2.1	.7	2.90	2.90	.831
[Chi-Square 3.4, Significance .633]										

TABLE 3 (Continued)

Skill	Group	Strongly Disagree (1)	Disagree (2)	Neutral (3)	Agree (4)	Strongly Agree (5)	Can't Evaluate	Median (1-5)	Mean (1-5)	SD (1-5)
Paragraph Development	CPA	3.0%	37.9%	43.9%	9.1%	4.5%	1.5%	2.69	2.74	.853
	IND	2.6	20.8	49.4	23.4	0	3.9	3.00	2.97	.758
	TOTAL	2.8	28.7	46.9	16.8	2.1	2.8	2.87	2.86	.809
	[Chi-Square 12.4, Significance .030]									
Use of Visual Aids	CPA	4.5	16.7	56.1	7.6	0	15.2	2.88	2.79	.680
	IND	5.2	18.2	49.4	18.2	0	9.1	2.95	2.89	.790
	TOTAL	4.9	17.5	52.4	13.3	0	11.9	2.91	2.84	.742
	[Chi-Square 4.5, Significance .344]									

strated. The disagree and neutral ratings received the majority of responses for most items.

Most of the skills were rated lower by the CPAs than by the industrial accountants. These results suggest again that communications skills are relatively more important and perhaps more closely analyzed by public practitioners. Only reading speed, correct grammar, and paragraph development demonstrated statistically significant differences between the two groups of practitioners.

Comparison of Needed and Demonstrated Skills

Results of the communications skills inventory demonstrate that these skills are needed but that performance in most of these skills can be improved. While a rather obvious discrepancy between need and performance is observable for nearly all skills, a few warrant special consideration.

Several of the skills which were ranked high in the needed skills analysis were ranked particularly low in the displayed skills analysis. These include memorandum and informal report writing and all of the mechanical skills of grammar, punctuation, and spelling. Conciseness in verbal presentation also demonstrated a large discrepancy. These differences may signal specific areas where additional emphasis should be placed in accounting curricula.

Consideration of the teaching methods used in most accounting courses might suggest that these are skills which generally do not receive specific attention in accounting courses or are not likely to be developed in these courses. In contrast, skills such as reading comprehension, and listening attentiveness and responsiveness received the highest performance ratings. These are skills which accounting programs probably stress and assist in developing.

Academicians' Perceptions of Needed Skills

The same inventory of communications skills was provided in the questionnaire mailed to accounting department administrators as in that mailed to practitioners. The results of the inventory relative to skills needed by staff accountants are shown in Table 4. As was the case with practitioners, academicians rated all of the skills as being needed by staff accountants. The medians ranged from 3.45 for use of visual aids to 4.88 for memorandums and informal reporting writing. Other than visual aids, all of the other items demonstrated medians larger than 4.0 for the entire sample of respondents. Standard deviations were slightly larger than in the practitioner sample, but the large majority of respondents indicated an "agree" or "strongly agree" response to all of the skills except visual aids.

The perceptions of the need for communications skills were similar across the three groups of respondents classified by the highest degree offered to accounting majors. Only reading comprehension demonstrated a statistically significant difference across groups. Respondents from schools offering only bachelor's degrees rated this skill more important than other respondents; however, this relatively higher rating from respondents from schools offering bachelor's degrees was not observed consistently for the list of skills. In general, differences across groups appear to be minor, and the type of degree program does not appear to be a major factor in explaining differences in the perceptions of academicians.

Academicians consistently rated the skills as being more important for staff accounting duties than did the combined sample of practitioners, and in nearly all cases, the academic responses were higher than for the CPA group. There was also a general agreement between skills considered most important by academicians and those considered most important by practitioners. Statistically significant differences between academicians and practitioners were observed for several of the skills (see Table 6). In each case, the academicians rated the skills as being more important than did the practitioners. These results suggest that academicians, on average, do not underestimate the importance of these skills and are aware of the need for the skills in the profession.

Academicians' Perceptions of Demonstrated Skills

Academicians were requested to express opinions concerning whether accounting graduates adequately demonstrated the skills listed in the inventory. Results are shown in Table 5. Medians range from a low of 2.42 for memorandums and informal report writing and formal oral presentation to a high of 3.74 for listening attentiveness. Ten of the skills demonstrate medians of less than 3.0 for the total sample of respondents and the majority of responses were "disagree,"

ACADEMICIANS' PERCEPTIONS OF COMMUNICATIONS SKILLS NEEDED BY STAFF ACCOUNTANTS

Skill	Group	Strongly Disagree (1)	Disagree (2)	Neutral (3)	Agree (4)	Strongly Agree (5)	Can't Evaluate	Median (1-5)	Mean (1-5)	SD (1-5)
Correspondence Writing	Bachelors	0%	2.9%	14.7%	35.3%	47.1%	0%	4.42	4.27	.828
	Masters	2.0	2.0	8.0	44.0	42.0	2.0	4.34	4.25	.855
	Doctorate	3.6	0	10.7	39.3	42.9	3.6	4.36	4.22	.934
	Total	1.8	1.8	10.7	40.2	43.8	1.8	4.37	4.25	.859
	[Chi-Square 3.3, Significance .912]									
Memorandums and Informal Report Writing	Bachelors	2.9	2.9	5.9	14.7	73.5	0	4.82	4.53	.961
	Masters	0	2.0	0	16.0	80.0	2.0	4.89	4.78	.550
	Doctorate	3.6	0	0	7.1	85.7	3.6	4.94	4.78	.801
	Total	1.8	1.8	1.8	13.4	79.5	1.8	4.88	4.70	.761
	[Chi-Square 8.2, Significance .419]									
Formal Report Writing	Bachelors	2.9	2.9	17.6	35.3	41.2	0	4.25	4.09	.996
	Masters	2.0	4.0	6.0	40.0	46.0	2.0	4.43	4.27	.908
	Doctorate	3.6	0	14.3	35.7	46.4	0	4.40	4.21	.957
	Total	2.7	2.7	11.6	37.5	44.6	0.9	4.37	4.20	.942
	[Chi-Square 4.1, Significance .845]									
Reading Speed	Bachelors	0	2.9	14.7	41.2	41.2	0	4.29	4.21	.808
	Masters	0	6.0	24.0	46.0	22.0	2.0	3.91	3.86	.842
	Doctorate	0	3.6	10.7	53.6	21.4	10.7	4.07	4.04	.735
	Total	0	4.5	17.9	46.4	27.7	3.6	4.06	4.01	.815
	[Chi-Square 6.8, Significance .388]									
Reading Comprehension	Bachelors	2.9	0	2.9	2.9	91.2	0	4.95	4.79	.770
	Masters	0	0	0	28.0	70.0	2.0	4.80	4.71	.456
	Doctorate	3.6	0	0	25.0	67.9	3.6	4.79	4.59	.844
	Total	1.8	0	0.9	19.6	75.9	1.8	4.85	4.71	.668
	[Chi-Square 12.3, Significance .055]									

TABLE 4 (Continued)

Skill	Group	Strongly Disagree (1)	Disagree (2)	Neutral (3)	Agree (4)	Strongly Agree (5)	Can't Evaluate	Median (1-5)	Mean (1-5)	SD (1-5)
Informal Oral Presentation	Bachelors	2.9%	0%	5.9%	29.4%	61.8%	0%	4.69	4.47	.861
	Masters	0	0	2.0	40.8	55.1	2.0	4.61	4.54	.544
	Doctorate	3.6	0	3.6	25.0	67.9	0	4.76	4.54	.881
	Total	1.8	0	3.6	33.3	60.4	0.9	4.68	4.52	.739
	[Chi-Square 4.5, Significance .604]									
Formal Oral Presentation	Bachelors	2.9	5.9	11.8	47.1	32.4	0	4.13	4.00	.985
	Masters	2.0	4.1	18.4	44.9	28.6	2.0	4.05	3.96	.922
	Doctorate	3.6	7.1	21.4	39.3	28.6	0	3.96	3.82	1.056
	Total	2.7	5.4	17.1	44.1	29.7	0.9	4.05	3.94	.976
	[Chi-Square 1.7, Significance .988]									
Listening Attentiveness	Bachelors	2.9	0	0	20.6	76.5	0	4.85	4.68	.768
	Masters	0	0	0	30.6	67.3	2.0	4.77	4.69	.468
	Doctorate	3.6	0	3.6	21.4	71.4	0	4.80	4.57	.879
	Total	1.8	0	0.9	25.2	71.2	0.9	4.80	4.66	.683
	[Chi-Square 6.0, Significance .428]									
Listening Responsiveness	Bachelors	3.0	0	3.0	18.2	69.7	6.1	4.83	4.61	.844
	Masters	0	0	0	38.8	57.1	4.1	4.66	4.60	.496
	Doctorate	3.6	0	3.6	28.6	60.7	3.6	4.71	4.48	.893
	Total	1.8	0	1.8	30.0	61.8	4.5	4.73	4.57	.719
	[Chi-Square 6.9, Significance .334]									
Correct Grammar	Bachelors	2.9	0	5.9	23.5	67.6	0	4.76	4.53	.861
	Masters	0	0	2.0	24.0	72.0	2.0	4.82	4.71	.500
	Doctorate	3.6	0	0	14.3	82.1	0	4.89	4.71	.810
	Total	1.8	0	2.7	21.4	73.2	0.9	4.82	4.66	.707
	[Chi-Square 5.1, Significance .531]									

TABLE 4 (Continued)

Skill	Group	Strongly Disagree (1)	Disagree (2)	Neutral (3)	Agree (4)	Strongly Agree (5)	Can't Evaluate	Median (1-5)	Mean (1-5)	SD (1-5)
Correct Punctuation	Bachelors	2.9%	0%	8.8%	35.3%	52.9%	0%	4.56	4.35	.884
	Masters	0	0	6.0	32.0	60.0	2.0	4.68	4.55	.614
	Doctorate	3.6	0	7.1	17.9	71.4	0	4.80	4.54	.922
	Total	1.8	0	7.1	29.5	60.7	0.9	4.68	4.49	.785
	[Chi-Square 4.5, Significance .610]									
Correct Spelling	Bachelors	2.9	0	8.8	26.5	61.8	0	4.69	4.44	.894
	Masters	0	2.0	6.0	22.0	68.0	2.0	4.78	4.59	.705
	Doctorate	3.6	3.6	0	21.4	71.4	0	4.80	4.54	.962
	Total	1.8	1.8	5.4	23.2	67.0	0.9	4.76	4.53	.829
	[Chi-Square 5.5, Significance .705]									
Outline Development	Bachelors	0	8.8	14.7	29.4	47.1	0	4.40	4.15	.989
	Masters	0	2.0	6.0	42.0	48.0	2.0	4.48	4.39	.702
	Doctorate	3.6	3.6	3.6	39.3	50.0	0	4.50	4.29	.976
	Total	0.9	4.5	8.0	37.5	48.2	0.9	4.46	4.29	.867
	[Chi-Square 8.9, Significance .353]									
Inductive Reasoning	Bachelors	2.9	2.9	2.9	35.3	55.9	0	4.61	4.38	.922
	Masters	0	2.0	0	50.0	46.0	2.0	4.44	4.43	.612
	Doctorate	3.6	0	7.1	21.4	67.9	0	4.76	4.50	.923
	Total	1.8	1.8	2.7	38.4	54.5	0.9	4.59	4.43	.793
	[Chi-Square 11.4, Significance .182]									
Deductive Reasoning	Bachelors	2.9	0	2.9	38.2	55.9	0	4.61	4.44	.824
	Masters	0	2.0	2.0	52.0	42.0	2.0	4.37	4.37	.636
	Doctorate	3.6	0	3.6	32.1	60.7	0	4.68	4.46	.881
	Total	1.8	0.9	2.7	42.9	50.9	0.9	4.53	4.41	.756
	[Chi-Square 6.4, Significance .599]									

TABLE 4 (Continued)

Skill	Group	Strongly Disagree (1)	Disagree (2)	Neutral (3)	Agree (4)	Strongly Agree (5)	Can't Evaluate	Median (1-5)	Mean (1-5)	SD (1-5)
Coherence in Verbal Presentation	Bachelors	0%	2.9%	0%	29.4%	67.6%	0%	4.76	4.62	.652
	Masters	0	0	2.0	30.0	66.0	2.0	4.76	4.65	.522
	Doctorate	3.6	0	0	25.0	71.4	0	4.80	4.61	.832
	Total	0.9	0.9	0.9	28.6	67.9	0.9	4.77	4.63	.646
	[Chi-Square 6.7, Significance .565]									
Clarity in Verbal Presentation	Bachelors	0	0	0	23.5	73.5	0	4.82	4.68	.638
	Masters	0	2.9	0	32.0	66.0	2.0	4.76	4.67	.474
	Doctorate	3.6	0	0	25.0	71.4	0	4.80	4.61	.832
	Total	0.9	0.9	0	27.7	69.6	0.9	4.79	4.66	.625
	[Chi-Square 6.1, Significance .417]									
Conciseness in Verbal Presentation	Bachelors	0	2.9	0	35.3	61.8	0	4.69	4.56	.660
	Masters	0	0	4.0	42.0	51.0	2.0	4.56	4.49	.582
	Doctorate	3.6	0	3.6	32.1	60.7	0	4.68	4.46	.881
	Total	0.9	0.9	2.7	37.5	57.1	0.9	4.63	4.51	.686
	[Chi-Square 7.5, Significance .482]									
Paragraph Development	Bachelors	0	2.9	5.9	41.2	47.1	2.9	4.46	4.36	.742
	Masters	2.0	2.0	10.0	46.0	38.0	2.0	4.26	4.18	.858
	Doctorate	3.6	0	3.6	50.0	39.3	3.6	4.32	4.26	.859
	Total	1.8	1.8	7.1	45.5	41.1	2.7	4.33	4.26	.821
	[Chi-Square 4.0, Significance .853]									
Use of Visual Aids	Bachelors	0	2.9	44.1	35.3	11.8	5.9	3.50	3.59	.756
	Masters	4.0	14.0	40.0	24.0	16.0	2.0	3.28	3.35	1.052
	Doctorate	3.6	7.1	28.6	32.1	25.0	3.6	3.79	3.70	1.068
	Total	2.7	8.9	38.4	29.5	17.0	3.6	3.45	3.51	.981
	[Chi-Square 8.3, Significance .406]									

"neutral," or "agree" for all items. There were no observable differences across groups of respondents based on highest degree offered.

Differences were observable between academic and practitioner groups, although these differences were not systematic. Fourteen of the skills indicated statistically significant differences in responses between these groups. However, these differences must be tempered by the larger number of "can't evaluate" responses received from academicians and by the lack of consistency in relative ratings between academics and practitioners. Correspondence writing, reading comprehension, informal oral presentation, listening attentiveness, listening responsiveness, correct grammar, correct punctuation, and outline development received higher ratings by academicians than practitioners (based on medians). On the other hand, memorandum and informal report writing, reading speed, formal oral presentation, coherence in verbal presentation, conciseness in verbal presentation, and paragraph development received lower ratings.

As was true of practitioners, academicians perceived several of the skills which they rated to be most important as also being most deficient. These items also agreed with practitioner assessments and included memorandum and informal report writing, and correct grammar, punctuation, and spelling.

Academicians were also asked their perceptions of the average quality of the communications skills demonstrated by accounting graduates from their respective programs. Table 7 shows that responses to this question were consistent with responses to the skills inventory. Half of the respondents indicate the level of skills was satisfactory while approximately an equal number marked the good and poor responses. These results confirm the previous analysis which indicated that communications skills are perceived to be adequate by a large number of academicians, but the average graduate is perceived to be proficient in these skills by few.

TABLE 5

ACADEMICIANS' PERCEPTIONS OF COMMUNICATIONS SKILLS DEMONSTRATED BY ACCOUNTING GRADUATES

Skill	Group	Strongly Disagree (1)	Disagree (2)	Neutral (3)	Agree (4)	Strongly Agree (5)	Can't Evaluate	Median (1-5)	Mean (1-5)	SD (1-5)
Correspondence Writing	Bachelors	0%	51.5%	15.2%	24.2%	0%	9.1%	2.38	2.70	.877
	Masters	4.3	46.8	21.3	17.0	2.1	8.5	2.39	2.63	.926
	Doctorate	7.1	35.7	39.3	10.7	0	7.1	2.59	2.58	.809
	Total	3.7	45.4	24.1	17.6	0.9	8.3	2.43	2.64	.874
	[Chi-Square 10.1, Significance .260]									
Memorandums and Informal Report Writing	Bachelors	0	47.1	14.7	26.5	2.9	8.8	2.47	2.84	.969
	Masters	4.2	50.0	8.3	27.1	2.1	8.3	2.33	2.71	1.025
	Doctorate	7.1	39.3	25.0	25.0	0	3.6	2.57	2.70	.183
	Total	3.6	46.4	14.5	26.4	1.8	7.3	2.42	2.75	.982
	[Chi-Square 6.8, Significance .563]									
Formal Report Writing	Bachelors	5.9	35.3	23.5	29.4	0	5.9	2.75	2.81	.965
	Masters	16.7	41.7	12.5	20.8	2.1	6.3	2.23	2.47	1.100
	Doctorate	7.1	39.3	39.3	7.1	3.6	3.6	2.55	2.59	.888
	Total	10.9	39.1	22.7	20.0	1.8	5.5	2.43	2.61	1.009
	[Chi-Square 13.2, Significance .104]									
Reading Speed	Bachelors	0	14.7	47.1	11.8	5.9	20.6	3.03	3.11	.801
	Masters	8.3	20.8	22.9	29.2	4.2	14.6	3.09	3.00	1.095
	Doctorate	7.1	7.1	46.4	25.0	0	14.3	3.12	3.04	.859
	Total	5.5	15.5	36.4	22.7	3.6	16.4	3.08	3.04	.948
	[Chi-Square 13.3, Significance .101]									
Reading Comprehension	Bachelors	2.9	17.6	29.4	26.5	8.8	14.7	3.25	3.24	1.023
	Masters	4.2	16.7	20.8	45.8	4.2	8.3	3.59	3.32	.983
	Doctorate	7.1	14.3	28.6	32.1	7.1	10.7	3.31	3.20	1.080
	Total	4.5	16.4	25.5	36.4	6.4	10.9	3.43	3.27	1.011
	[Chi-Square 4.7, Significance .786]									

TABLE 5 (Continued)

Skill	Group	Strongly Disagree (1)	Disagree (2)	Neutral (3)	Agree (4)	Strongly Agree (5)	Can't Evaluate	Median (1-5)	Mean (1-5)	SD (1-5)
Informal Oral Presentation	Bachelors	2.9%	17.6%	20.6%	41.2%	11.8%	5.9%	3.64	3.44	1.045
	Masters	8.7	28.3	17.4	37.0	2.2	6.5	3.06	2.95	1.090
	Doctorate	11.1	11.1	33.3	40.7	0	3.7	3.28	3.08	1.017
	Total	7.5	20.6	22.4	39.3	4.7	5.6	3.35	3.14	1.068
	[Chi-Square 11.8, Significance .159]									
Formal Oral Presentation	Bachelors	2.9	23.5	29.4	29.4	0	14.7	3.05	3.00	.886
	Masters	10.6	48.9	19.1	14.9	0	6.4	2.24	2.41	.897
	Doctorate	14.3	42.9	14.3	21.4	0	7.1	2.25	2.46	1.029
	Total	9.2	39.4	21.1	21.1	0	9.2	2.42	2.60	.957
	[Chi-Square 10.4, Significance .110]									
Listening Attentiveness	Bachelors	2.9	14.7	20.6	47.1	5.9	8.8	3.66	3.42	.958
	Masters	2.1	4.3	17.0	59.6	6.4	10.6	3.86	3.71	.774
	Doctorate	7.4	14.8	22.2	51.9	3.7	0	3.61	3.30	1.031
	Total	3.7	10.2	19.4	53.7	5.6	7.4	3.74	3.51	.916
	[Chi-Square 5.9, Significance .658]									
Listening Responsiveness	Bachelors	3.0	12.1	18.2	48.5	3.0	15.2	3.69	3.43	.920
	Masters	2.1	10.6	25.5	51.1	0	10.6	3.63	3.41	.798
	Doctorate	7.4	18.5	25.9	40.7	0	7.4	3.29	3.08	.997
	Total	3.7	13.1	23.4	47.7	0.9	11.2	3.59	3.33	.893
	[Chi-Square 5.3, Significance .728]									
Correct Grammar	Bachelors	5.9	32.4	20.6	32.4	5.9	2.9	3.00	3.00	1.090
	Masters	10.4	27.1	20.8	29.2	6.3	6.3	2.95	2.93	1.156
	Doctorate	10.7	17.9	39.3	28.6	0	3.6	3.00	2.89	.974
	Total	9.1	26.4	25.5	30.0	4.5	4.5	2.98	2.94	1.082
	[Chi-Square 5.8, Significance .665]									

TABLE 5 (Continued)

Skill	Group	Strongly Disagree (1)	Disagree (2)	Neutral (3)	Agree (4)	Strongly Agree (5)	Can't Evaluate	Median (1-5)	Mean (1-5)	SD (1-5)
Correct Punctuation	Bachelors	2.9%	35.3%	26.5%	32.4%	0%	2.9%	2.89	2.91	.914
	Masters	12.5	29.2	20.8	29.2	2.1	6.3	2.75	2.78	1.106
	Doctorate	10.7	17.9	35.7	32.1	0	3.6	3.05	2.93	.997
	Total	9.1	28.2	26.4	30.9	0.9	4.5	2.90	2.86	1.014
	[Chi-Square 5.3, Significance .720]									
Correct Spelling	Bachelors	5.9	32.4	26.5	32.4	0	2.9	2.89	2.88	.960
	Masters	8.3	29.2	25.0	29.2	2.1	6.3	2.88	2.87	1.036
	Doctorate	10.7	17.9	39.3	28.6	0	3.6	3.00	2.89	.974
	Total	8.2	27.3	29.1	30.0	0.9	4.5	2.92	2.88	.987
	[Chi-Square 4.8, Significance .782]									
Outline Development	Bachelors	3.0	24.2	33.3	27.3	0	12.1	3.00	2.97	.865
	Masters	6.3	22.9	22.9	29.2	8.3	10.4	3.18	3.12	1.117
	Doctorate	7.1	21.4	32.1	28.6	3.6	7.1	3.06	3.00	1.020
	Total	5.5	22.9	28.4	28.4	4.6	10.1	3.08	3.94	1.015
	[Chi-Square 4.8, Significance .779]									
Inductive Reasoning	Bachelors	5.9	17.6	44.1	23.5	2.9	5.9	3.03	3.00	.916
	Masters	2.1	20.8	29.2	39.6	0	8.3	3.29	3.16	.861
	Doctorate	7.1	10.7	42.9	35.7	0	3.6	3.21	3.11	.892
	Total	4.5	17.3	37.3	33.6	0.9	6.4	3.17	3.10	.880
	[Chi-Square 7.5, Significance .479]									
Deductive Reasoning	Bachelors	5.9	17.6	35.3	32.4	2.9	5.9	3.17	3.09	.963
	Masters	4.2	16.7	31.3	37.5	2.1	8.3	3.30	3.18	.922
	Doctorate	7.1	7.1	50.0	32.1	0	3.6	3.18	3.11	.847
	Total	5.5	14.5	37.3	34.5	1.8	6.4	3.22	3.14	.908

Skill	Group	Strongly Disagree (1)	Disagree (2)	Neutral (3)	Agree (4)	Strongly Agree (5)	Can't Evaluate	Median (1-5)	Mean (1-5)	SD (1-5)
Coherence in Verbal Presentation	Bachelors	2.9%	32.4%	17.6%	44.1%	0%	2.9%	3.25	3.06	.966
	Masters	8.3	20.8	22.9	35.4	4.2	8.3	3.23	3.07	1.087
	Doctorate	10.7	7.1	46.4	32.1	3.6	0	3.19	3.11	.994
	Total	7.3	20.9	27.3	37.3	2.7	4.5	3.22	3.08	1.016
	[Chi-Square 13.7, Significance .091]									
Clarity in Verbal Presentation	Bachelors	2.9	32.4	23.5	38.2	0	2.9	3.06	3.00	.935
	Masters	6.3	20.8	31.3	29.2	4.2	8.3	3.10	3.05	1.011
	Doctorate	7.1	14.3	50.0	28.6	0	0	3.07	3.00	.861
	Total	5.5	22.7	33.6	31.8	1.8	4.5	3.08	3.02	.940
	[Chi-Square 8.5, Significance .384]									
Conciseness in Verbal Presentation	Bachelors	5.9	26.5	38.2	23.5	2.9	2.9	2.92	2.91	.947
	Masters	10.4	25.0	33.3	20.8	2.1	8.3	2.81	2.77	1.008
	Doctorate	14.3	25.0	39.3	21.4	0	0	2.77	2.68	.983
	Total	10.0	25.5	36.4	21.8	1.8	4.5	2.84	2.79	.978
	[Chi-Square 1.3, Significance .996]									
Paragraph Development	Bachelors	5.9	29.4	35.3	14.7	0	14.7	2.71	2.69	.850
	Masters	10.4	29.2	31.3	16.7	4.2	8.3	2.70	2.73	1.042
	Doctorate	10.7	25.0	42.9	17.9	0	3.6	2.79	2.70	.912
	Total	9.1	28.2	35.5	16.4	1.8	9.1	2.73	2.71	.946
	[Chi-Square 4.1, Significance .850]									
Use of Visual Aids	Bachelors	5.9	23.5	29.4	14.7	0	26.5	2.75	2.72	.891
	Masters	12.5	10.4	43.8	10.4	0	22.9	2.86	2.68	.915
	Doctorate	7.1	17.9	50.0	10.7	—	14.3	2.86	2.75	.794
	Total	9.1	16.4	40.9	11.8	0	21.8	2.83	2.71	.866
	[Chi-Square 4.7, Significance .582]									

TABLE 6

TESTS OF DIFFERENCES BETWEEN PRACTITIONERS' AND ACADEMICIANS' PERCEPTIONS OF NEEDED AND DEMONSTRATED COMMUNICATIONS SKILLS

Skill	Needed		Demonstrated	
	Chi-Square	Significance	Chi-Square	Significance
Correspondence Writing	4.9	.425	9.8	.082
Memorandum and Informal Report Writing	23.3	.0003	11.6	.041
Formal Report Writing	7.3	.202	4.8	.439
Reading Speed	9.4	.094	16.8	.005
Reading Comprehension	11.0	.027	9.9	.079
Informal Oral Presentation	9.6	.087	20.1	.001
Formal Oral Presentation	11.3	.046	10.1	.074
Listening Attentiveness	4.4	.355	10.4	.065
Listening Responsiveness	5.8	.218	14.1	.015
Correct Grammar	9.0	.109	13.6	.018
Correct Punctuation	9.5	.092	11.2	.048
Correct Spelling	8.9	.113	6.3	.282
Outline Development	7.7	.171	11.0	.051
Inductive Reasoning	5.4	.375	7.7	.174
Deductive Reasoning	3.7	.597	6.4	.268
Coherence in Verbal Presentation	14.5	.013	10.3	.068
Clarity in Verbal Presentation	14.7	.012	6.5	.260
Conciseness in Verbal Presentation	7.6	.177	10.9	.054
Paragraph Development	15.8	.008	10.6	.060
Use of Visual Aids	6.8	.237	6.9	.140

TABLE 7

ACADEMICIANS' PERCEPTIONS OF AVERAGE QUALITY OF
ACCOUNTING GRADUATES' COMMUNICATIONS SKILLS

Quality	Percent Response
Very Good	.9
Good	24.6
Satisfactory	50.0
Poor	20.2
Very Poor	3.5
Can't Evaluate	.9

Summary

Differences in perceptions of communications skills needed and demonstrated by staff level accountants appear to be minimal across groups of practitioners and academicians. The majority of respondents agreed that the skills listed in the inventory were needed for successful completion of staff accountant duties, and a majority indicated that they perceived that staff accountants demonstrated less than adequate proficiency in many of these skills. The greatest dissatisfaction was shown with writing and mechanical skills (grammar, spelling, and punctuation).

Four

The Effect of Deficiencies in Communications Skills on the Behavior of Practicing Accountants

In order to assess further the importance of communications skills for staff accountants, practicing accountants were asked about the role of the skills in hiring and dismissal practices. Information about these practices is also useful for assessing whether deficiencies in communications skills are likely to affect staff accounting personnel. A summary of the responses to these questions is shown in Table 8.

Practitioners were asked to indicate the frequency with which communications skills deficiencies were a primary or contributing reason for not hiring or for dismissing staff accounting personnel. These deficiencies were more frequently a reason for not hiring a person than for dismissal. While communications skills deficiencies appear to be a frequent contributing reason for not hiring a person, they are seldom a primary reason for dismissing someone.

"Sometimes" was the answer which received the most frequent response for the primary reason for not hiring question. "Frequently" received the most responses for the contributing reason for not hiring question. "Not often" was the most popular response for the primary reason for dismissal question, while "sometimes" was most popular for the contributing reason for dismissal question.

It is logical that deficiencies would be a more frequent reason for not hiring than for dismissal since the majority of persons with major deficiencies should have been screened out during the interview process and would not have been hired.

In general, the responses to these questions indicate that communications skills deficiencies are an important consideration in hiring

TABLE 8

PRACTITIONERS' PERCEPTIONS OF FREQUENCY OF OCCASIONS IN WHICH COMMUNICATIONS SKILLS INFLUENCE HIRING AND DISMISSAL PRACTICES

Situation	Group	Very Frequently (1)	Frequently (2)	Sometimes (3)	Not Often (4)	Never (5)	Can't Evaluate	Median (1-5)	Mean (1-5)	SD (1-5)
Primary Reason for Not Hiring	CPA	10.6%	24.2%	40.9%	16.7%	3.0%	4.5%	2.82	2.76	.979
	IND	3.9	18.2	42.9	26.0	3.9	5.2	3.09	3.08	.894
	TOTAL	7.0	21.0	42.0	21.7	3.5	4.9	2.97	2.93	.944
	[Chi-Square 4.5, Significance .484]									
Contributing Reason for Not Hiring	CPA	23.4	31.3	26.6	9.4	4.7	4.7	2.28	2.37	1.113
	IND	13.2	39.5	35.5	7.9	2.6	1.3	2.42	2.47	.920
	TOTAL	17.9	35.7	31.4	8.6	3.6	2.9	2.36	2.43	1.008
	[Chi-Square 5.5, Significance .360]									
Primary Reason for Dismissal	CPA	4.8	6.3	25.4	46.0	7.9	9.5	3.69	3.51	.947
	IND	0	3.9	18.4	31.6	34.2	11.8	4.19	4.09	.883
	TOTAL	2.2	5.0	21.6	38.1	22.3	10.8	3.92	3.82	.955
	[Chi-Square 17.5, Significance .004]									
Contributing Reason for Dismissal	CPA	4.6	21.5	36.9	26.2	3.1	7.7	3.04	3.02	.930
	IND	1.3	13.2	30.3	32.9	13.2	9.2	3.52	3.48	.964
	TOTAL	2.8	17.0	33.3	29.8	8.5	8.5	3.28	3.26	.972
	[Chi-Square 8.1, Significance .153]									

practices and that these deficiencies frequently contribute to a decision not to hire an individual. Public practitioners indicated that these deficiencies were more frequent factors in all of the decisions examined. These results are consistent with those of the skills inventory which indicated that communications skills were important for staff accountants and that public practitioners generally perceive the skills to be somewhat more important than the industrial accountants.

Practitioners were also asked to identify the skills which most frequently contributed to decisions not to hire or to dismiss a person. Table 9 indicates responses to these questions. Results are consistent to a large extent with responses to the skills inventory. The skills listed most frequently were those which were perceived to be most needed (Table 2) and which were perceived to be most deficient (Table 3).

Clarity in verbal presentation received the most responses for the decision-not-to-hire question (32 percent of all respondents indicated this item). Grammar, listening skills and coherence and conciseness also were marked frequently, although listening responsiveness, coherence and clarity were indicated more frequently by industrial accountants than by CPAs. Also, it is apparent that the skills which received the most frequent responses were those which can be assessed readily in an interview situation.

Responses for the decision-to-dismiss question were more uniform across skills than were the previous responses. Firms can assess more readily the range of skills after an individual is hired. Again, the results are consistent with the skills inventory. In addition to those items frequently marked in the previous question, memorandum and informal report writing, and reasoning skills were marked frequently. Formal report writing also received a number of responses, although more responses were received from the CPAs than the industrial accountants.

The major differences between the responses to these questions and responses to the skills inventory appear in the punctuation and spelling items. These skills were marked as being important and frequently deficient but were not noted as being major factors in hiring and dismissal practices. A possible explanation for this phenomenon may be that while deficiencies exist in these skills, secretarial and clerical staffs are available, in many cases, to correct these problems.

Practitioners were also asked whether they perceived any changes in the proficiency of communications skills demonstrated by staff accountants. Table 10 indicates that the perceptions of CPAs and industrial accounts were similar, but that there was little consensus among

PRACTITIONERS' PERCEPTIONS OF COMMUNICATIONS SKILLS DEFICIENCIES
WHICH RESULT IN NOT HIRING OR DISMISSING STAFF ACCOUNTANTS

Skill	Decision Not to Hire			Chi-Square (Significance)	Decision to Dismiss			Chi-Square (Significance)
	CPA	IND	TOTAL		CPA	IND	TOTAL	
Correspondence Writing	7.5%	6.3%	6.8%	.07 (.787)	9.0%	5.1%	6.8%	.86 (.354)
Memo and Informal Reports	4.5	2.5	3.4	.42 (.519)	10.4	19.0	15.1	2.1 (.151)
Formal Reports	6.0	1.3	3.4	2.4 (.119)	22.4	11.4	16.4	3.2 (.074)
Reading Speed	0	0	0	—	0	1.3	.7	.86 (.355)
Reading Comprehension	3.0	1.3	2.1	.53 (.466)	4.5	3.8	4.1	.04 (.837)
Informal Oral Presentation	22.4	29.1	26.0	.85 (.356)	14.9	15.2	15.1	.002 (.965)
Formal Oral Presentation	4.5	0	2.1	3.6 (.051)	7.5	7.6	7.5	.001 (.976)
Listening Attentiveness	19.4	21.5	20.5	.10 (.753)	14.9	12.7	13.7	.158 (.692)
Listening Responsiveness	13.4	31.6	23.3	6.7 (.010)	11.9	12.7	12.3	.02 (.895)
Correct Grammar	20.9	27.8	24.7	.94 (.331)	10.4	6.3	8.2	.82 (.367)

TABLE 9 (Continued)

Skill	Decision Not to Hire			Chi-Square (Significance)	Decision to Dismiss			Chi-Square (Significance)
	CPA	IND	TOTAL		CPA	IND	TOTAL	
Correct Punctuation	3.0%	3.8%	3.4%	.07 (.788)	7.5%	1.3%	4.1%	3.5 (.060)
Correct Spelling	4.5	5.1	4.8	.03 (.869)	7.5	3.8	5.5	.94 (.332)
Outline Development	1.5	2.5	2.1	.19 (.659)	7.5	7.6	7.5	.001 (.976)
Inductive Reasoning	7.5	8.9	8.2	.09 (.759)	16.4	12.7	14.4	.416 (.519)
Deductive Reasoning	6.0	8.9	7.5	.43 (.510)	20.9	13.9	17.1	1.2 (.265)
Coherence	19.4	39.2	30.1	6.8 (.009)	13.4	16.5	15.1	.26 (.611)
Clarity	22.4	40.5	32.2	5.5 (.020)	10.4	17.7	14.4	1.6 (.212)
Conciseness	17.9	24.1	21.2	.82 (.366)	9.0	11.4	10.3	.234 (.629)
Paragraph Development	3.0	0	1.4	2.4 (.122)	6.0	6.3	6.2	.008 (.928)
Visual Aids	0	0	0	—	0	1.3	.7	.85 (.355)

Note: Percentages refer to the ratio of the number of reponses to the item to the total number of respondents.

either group of respondents. While these responses are not particularly helpful in assessing whether accounting programs or university education has development of these skills, the responses do suggest that deficiencies which are perceived to exist are not being improved at a sufficiently rapid pace to be apparent to the majority of practitioners.

TABLE 10

PRACTITIONERS' PERCEPTIONS OF LONGITUDINAL CHANGES IN
COMMUNICATIONS SKILLS DEMONSTRATED BY STAFF ACCOUNTANTS

Group	Increasing	Decreasing	Remaining Unchanged	Can't Evaluate
CPA	25.8%	30.3%	31.8%	12.1%
IND	20.5	26.9	35.9	16.7
TOTAL	22.9	28.5	34.0	14.6
[Chi-Square 1.3, Significance.740]				

A final question to practitioners involved the efforts being made by firms to improve the communications skills of their employees. Respondents were asked whether their firm had a formal program to improve communications skills. Results are shown in Table 11. Approximately 38 percent of the respondents from both CPA firms and private industries replied that formal programs do exist. These replies again suggest that communications skills are an important concern of practitioners and that the profession is not satisfied with the level of skills demonstrated by staff accountants.

If efforts are being expended by a large number of firms to improve communications skills, even after individuals with poor skills are screened out of the market, perhaps more emphasis should be placed on development of these skills by academic programs. Another objective of this study was to determine what efforts are being made currently by these programs to develop communications skills and whether the emphasis is increasing. The next section of this study examines these issues.

TABLE 11

COMPANIES REPORTING FORMAL PROGRAMS TO
IMPROVE EMPLOYEE COMMUNICATIONS SKILLS

Group	Program Exists	Program Does Not Exist	Not Sure
CPA	37.9%	59.1%	3.0%
IND	37.7	58.4	3.9
TOTAL	37.8	58.7	3.5
	[Chi-Square .08, Significance .961]		

Five

Efforts To Develop Communications Skills in Accounting Programs

A third objective of this research study was to examine efforts currently being made by academic programs to develop communications skills and prospective changes in these efforts. The results of the previous sections of the survey indicated that academicians perceive that communications skills are needed by accounting graduates and that deficiencies exist in the level of skills demonstrated by graduates. Accordingly, one would assume that accounting programs are giving some attention to the development of these skills. This expectation appears to be correct based on the following results.

Table 12 demonstrates that a majority of accounting programs have taken formal steps to develop skills among undergraduate students. More than half the responding schools indicated that communications courses (above general education requirements) are required of undergraduate accounting majors, and an additional 25 percent indicated that courses are recommended to these students. Course offerings at the graduate level are more restricted with only about 20 percent of the responding schools indicating required courses.

Of the courses in communications skills, few (less than five percent) are taught by accounting faculty. Nearly half of the courses are taught by business (other than accounting) faculty. Thus, one must assume that in many cases these courses are offered to students other than accounting majors and that the courses are not oriented specifically towards accounting.

Respondents also indicated the number of credit hours offered for communications courses. These responses were converted to a semester hour equivalent and averaged across schools offering courses.

TABLE 12

COURSE OFFERINGS IN COMMUNICATIONS SKILLS
ABOVE GENERAL EDUCATION REQUIREMENTS

Characteristics of Courses	Undergraduate Programs (n = 111)	Graduate Programs (n = 80)
Courses are Recommended to Majors	25.2%*	12.5%
Courses are Required of Majors	54.1%	21.3%
Courses are Taught by Accounting Faculty	4.5%	5.0%
Courses are Taught by Business (Nonaccounting) Faculty	38.8%	16.3%
Courses are Taught by Nonbusiness Faculty	36.0%	12.5%
Average Credit Offered per Program (Semester Equivalent)	3.5 hrs.	2.7 hrs.

*The percentage for each item is based on the ratio of the number of programs responding positively to that item to the total number of programs.

TABLE 13

REASONS COURSES IN COMMUNICATIONS SKILLS
ARE NOT OFFERED

Reason	Percent of Responses (n = 23)
Inadequate Marginal Benefits	4.3
Lack of Faculty Interest	26.1
Lack of Student Interest	13.0
Inadequate Resources	65.2
Insufficient Time in Program	78.3
Better Alternatives*	17.4

*All respondents indicated that assignments in accounting courses emphasized communications skills.

On average, schools with communications courses offer 3.5 hours credit to undergraduate students and 2.7 hours credit to graduate students for these courses. A single three-hour course was the response indicated by the majority of respondents.

Respondents from universities not offering communications courses were asked about the reasons for not offering these courses. Table 13 shows that the primary reasons perceived by the respondents were insufficient time in the program and inadequate resources. Few of these respondents expressed an opinion that courses would not be beneficial. Several indicated that they did not perceive special courses to be necessary since these skills were emphasized in other courses.

Since alternatives other than specialized courses exist for developing communications skills, academicians were asked to indicate their perceptions of the approximate percentage of total instructional hours devoted primarily to the development of these skills. As can be seen in Table 14, the average percent indicated was 6.2 for undergraduate programs and 9.1 percent for graduate. The higher percentage responses for graduate programs suggests that respondents perceive that efforts are being made to develop communications skills through activities other than specialized courses.

TABLE 14

PERCENTAGE OF INSTRUCTIONAL HOURS (ABOVE GENERAL
EDUCATIONAL REQUIREMENTS) DEVOTED PRIMARILY
TO COMMUNICATIONS SKILLS DEVELOPMENT

Program	Average Percent
Undergraduate	6.2
Graduate	9.1

It is logical that assignments in graduate courses (term papers, oral presentations) would require more attention to communications skills than typical assignments in undergraduate courses. On the other hand, the efforts currently being made in accounting programs to develop skills, whether formal or informal, do not appear to be especially significant. Certainly, there appears to be room to expand these efforts, especially if a trend to increase the hours required of accounting majors is developing.

Concern for insufficient time and inadequate resources are common among academicians, given the proliferation of accounting subject matter and the shortage of faculty. Thus, it is to be expected that communications skills, like most other subjects, may receive less attention than most academicians and practitioners would prefer. However, one might expect that as accounting programs and course offerings are expanded, additional consideration may be given to these skills.

Academicians were questioned concerning their perceptions of prospective changes in the emphasis placed on communications courses. Table 15 reveals that the large majority of respondents perceive an increase in emphasis on these skills in their programs. Very few respondents indicated a decreasing emphasis, reiterating the awareness and concern for needed skills.

TABLE 15

PERCEIVED CHANGE IN EMPHASIS ON COMMUNICATIONS
SKILLS IN ACCOUNTING PROGRAMS

Emphasis	Percent Response
Increasing	71.1
Decreasing	.9
Remaining Unchanged	28.1

Six

Towards Skills Development

If the discrepancy between accounting practitioners' assessments of communications skills needed and those demonstrated by their employees are to be taken seriously by accounting educators, it is evident that an increased emphasis on communications in the accounting curriculum is necessary. Accounting educators appear to be cognizant of both the discrepancy and the need for additional emphasis on communications skills. Given the results of the survey discussed previously, this chapter provides a brief analysis of several possible solutions to the problem of communications skills. The chapter is not intended to be an exhaustive analysis but rather to be an introduction which may stimulate thought and direct those concerned towards appropriate solutions. An objective of this study was not the development of curriculum materials but to explore possible solutions to an identified problem.

In general, there are at least three possible nonexclusive avenues which could be taken by an accounting program. One approach would be to modify existing accounting courses to provide more attention to communications skills, and another would be to develop special courses for skills development. A third approach would be to control the quality of skills demonstrated by students entering and exiting accounting programs without necessarily becoming directly involved with the development of communications skills.

Modifying Accounting Courses

Certainly, more attention to both written and oral communications in accounting courses would, to a degree, help in improving communications skills. Accounting courses, especially advanced courses, can be modified to include written and oral assignments. Considering the constant expansion of the body of accounting knowledge, however, and the limitations of time in any course, it is unreasonable to expect accounting instructors to devote appreciable effort to developing communications skills in their students. Neither is it reasonable to expect most accounting faculty to possess the expertise necessary to teach communications skills. The additional time and effort required to grade assignments for communications content and mechanics and to instruct students properly in these skills (especially in undergraduate classes with large numbers of students) is prohibitive. These drawbacks make this option doubtful as an exclusive method for solving communications problems. Furthermore, the kinds of generalized business communications courses taught at many universities are often oriented too much toward secretarial skills to meet the needs of increasingly professional accounting programs.

An Accounting Communications Course

Accordingly, we suggest that, in addition to placing more emphasis on communications skills in accounting courses, and in addition to available general business communications courses, other methods be considered for solving what appears to be a serious problem in the profession. With these factors in mind, the most viable alternative to meet the needs indicated in the responses to the survey appears to be a course or courses in pre-professional written and oral communications designed particularly to develop the skills most applicable to the job demands of accountants. Such courses would allow a much greater degree of quality control by accounting departments and would make particularly useful additions to expanded five-year professional accounting programs. In the following paragraphs, we will discuss a few of the more pertinent attributes and possible methods for teaching such a course.

When considering the development of communications courses for the accounting curriculum, it is important to recognize first of all that neither writing for accounting nor business writing in general is a field isolated or removed from basic expository prose. Technical and professional writing, of course, place special demands upon the writer, but these kinds of communications share underlying purposes with expository writing of any kind: to explain, to document, to persuade or convince. With only very minor exceptions resulting from the demands of subject matter, the kinds of writing in which practicing accountants need to be proficient are all sub-genres of exposition. For example, business correspondence most frequently employs techniques of persuasion and explanation; an auditor's working papers frequently include description of procedure and process analysis; memorandums require skills in concise explanatory writing and the ability to relate factual material clearly; reports might utilize any of the previously mentioned skills plus the ability to incorporate secondary source material (results of research, authoritative pronouncements, IRS code citations and their interpretations) and the ability to analyze and interpret observations (conclusions drawn from audit evidence).

Once the teacher of a communications course for accounting majors recognizes the applicability of these traditional rhetorical forms to the problems of business riting, it becomes clear that the types of writing emphasized by accounting practitioners in the survey (correspondence, memorandums, formal and informal reports) can best be taught as special applications of traditional rhetorical techniques. In each specific assignment, it is important to clarify for the student the relationship between his particular subject matter and the rhetorical form or forms most effective for successfully communicating that subject matter.

Accounting communications is an area of study particularly adaptable to the case method of instruction. In teaching correspondence writing, for example, a problem like the following might be assigned to the class:

> At a social function, you make contact with Mr. Henry Jones, owner of a small manufacturing company, who wants to engage the CPA firm by which you are employed to prepare his company's financial statements and tax returns. You are to write a memorandum to the managing partner of your firm describing your contact with Mr. Jones and the nature of the services he is seeking to have your firm perform. Remember to detail to the partner the steps you will take in setting up the services to the client. Next, assuming you are given a "go-ahead" by the partner and you and Jones have agreed upon the nature of the services, write an engagement letter to Jones. Be sure to consider any applicable Statements on Auditing Standards and the Code of Professional Ethics of CPAs; in particular, be sure to point out the distinction between your engagement, which involves preparation of accounting statements, and an engagement which would involve an audit of financial statements.

Such an assignment would incorporate the rhetorical techniques of description, process-analysis, definition, and explanation. It would also help to emphasize for the student the special problems of legal liability that accountants must frequently consider in their writing. An additional objective of this assignment would be to stress the importance of adapting the communication to varying audience levels. The memorandum to the managing partner would be written to a professional audience while the letter to Mr. Jones would not, thereby requiring an entirely different approach in order to ensure clarity of communication. Adapting writing to the audience is an important skill for accountants, who must be able to communicate on appropriate levels both within the profession and with clients of diverse experience and educational backgrounds. Finally, an assignment such as this, which calls for an inter-office memorandum and outside correspondence, would provide an opportunity to clarify for the student the distinctions between these two important forms of business communications.

Similar approaches could be used in teaching other forms of writing, such as reports and proposals. In each case, though, it is important that the writing assignment not be simply a variation on the standard college term paper, but, instead, be as similar to an on-the-job writing task as possible. Assignments should be designed to encourage students to imagine themselves as employed accountants faced with a "real-life" communications problem rather than an artificial, classroom task. In solving these communications problems, the student should learn to identify and apply the rhetorical techniques most suitable to the given situation.

Developing writing skills, though, is obviously not the only objective in a communications course for accounting majors. Though practitioners rated employees slightly higher in oral communications proficiency than written, oral communication should still be strongly emphasized in a communications course. Students should first realize that successful oral communications differ greatly in technique and presentation from written communications. One way to enforce this distinction is by having students prepare first a written report on a given subject and then, after the report has been submitted for grading, give an oral presentation of the results of the report and use visual aids. Of course, during the oral presentation the student should not be allowed to read the report, but, instead, should be limited to notes.

In addition to formal oral presentations, respondents to the survey also emphasized the importance of informal oral skills, listening attentiveness, and listening responsiveness. These skills are much more difficult to develop in a classroom situation than are more formal oral skills. However, one assignment which would incorporate all of the above-mentioned qualities is the interview. In this assignment a student might be instructed to set up an appointment with a local accounting professional to discuss a particular aspect of accounting (for example, accountants' legal liability or the problems of the historical cost concept.) Before conducting the interview, the student would have to generate a list of questions on the topic. During the interview listening attentiveness and responsiveness would come into play. As a final step in the assignment, the student would be required to present to the class an informal oral report on the results of the interview which was conducted. In addition to developing skills in oral communications, this assignment also could serve as a preliminary step in the preparation of a longer report to be submitted later in the semester.

Given the demonstrated need for improved communications skills for accounting graduates, it would appear beneficial for accounting departments to institute courses to meet this need. Existing business department courses (the majority of current offering appears to be of this type) are evidently not meeting this need. They are also unable, for the most part, to adapt to the specific requirements of accountants' writing, and they do not allow the opportunity for direct quality control by the accounting department. A course developed along the general outlines indicated above and taught by faculty with strong backgrounds in expository writing who could also relate rhetorical techniques to realistic accounting problems and situations could make a valuable contribution to the accounting curriculum.

An obvious problem with this alternative is the lack of available or trained faculty. Many accounting departments are already under-staffed and are struggling to cover current course requirements with qualified faculty. Likewise, the number of faculty members who are trained and interested in both accounting and communications may be limited.

On the other hand, several possible solutions to the problem exist. The type of course envisioned would be readily adaptable to a team-teaching approach. The team, consisting of someone trained in accounting and someone trained in communications, would cooperate in developing assignments and in assessing both the content and mechanics of the students' presentations. Cooperation with communications departments (*e.g.*, English and speech) would appear to be a feasible method for developing skills. These departments are sometimes overstaffed and generally are willing to develop service courses for special communications needs. After team teaching a course with accounting faculty a few times or after special study of the accounting process, it is feasible that communications faculty may become quite capable of teaching courses to accounting majors.

A number of universities are now providing business minors to students in humanities and social sciences. It is possible that specialists could be developed in the area of accounting communication or that accounting departments may hire a communications specialist who is trained or can be trained in accounting to cover these courses. A similar phenomenon has occurred to some extent with other specialized subjects needed by accounting students such as business law and computer science.

Entry and Exit Criteria

A final consideration which perhaps this study should pose is whether accounting programs should be involved in communications skills development. Educators could take the attitude that these skills are not directly related to accounting knowledge and are beyond the scope of the accounting program. Without arguing this point, it would seem that the current approach of training students in accounting without giving attention to their communications skills is a waste of resources. Students without at least a sufficient level of skills will have a difficult time in obtaining a job. At a minimum, it would appear that accounting educators should be aware of the skills demonstrated by individual students and attempt to reduce the number of students in accounting programs with inadequate skills.

One might question whether students who have completed twelve years of primary and secondary school and general education requirements in college communications and who have still not developed a fundamental grasp of the mechanics of the English language can be taught these skills in the accounting program. Since mechanical skills still appear to be a major deficiency of accounting graduates, perhaps entrance requirements into accounting programs should emphasize communications skills. Appropriate tests could be administered to evaluate these skills and satisfactory proficiency would be required for admission.

More responsibility for the development of skills also could be placed on students by requiring demonstrated proficiency in communications skills as a requirement for graduation. Students who could not demonstrate proficiency could be required to take remedial courses or simply could be denied a degree. These measures would help ensure that students who successfully completed accounting majors would be employable in their chosen field. While requiring proficiency as a graduation requirement might place the emphasis on skills development at the output rather than input end of the academic program, enforcement of the requirement might pose a barrier for entrance for students who realize they will have difficulty demonstrating proficiency. The requirement also would provide incentive for students enrolled in accounting programs to develop communications skills, but it would not prevent otherwise competent students from enrolling in the programs.

Conclusion

Each of the methods suggested for developing communications skills is only a partial solution. The problem is significant enough that a combination of these methods and perhaps others may be needed to provide a workable plan in any particular educational setting. Each accounting program is unique because of the particular mix of students, faculty, objectives, and resources available to it. Accordingly, a plan to develop communications skills in accounting students must be tailored to the specific program.

Appendix A

Letter to Practitioners

The American Accounting Association is sponsoring a project to determine the importance of communications skills for the performance of staff accountant duties. This project may be instrumental in identifying educational problems which warrant attention by college professors. Information concerning the importance of communications skills is being sought from individuals in industry and public practice who are directly involved in the supervision of accounting personnel and can evaluate the communications skills needed and demonstrated by practicing accountants.

You can be of assistance in this project in two ways: (1) by completing the enclosed questionnaire or by directing it to someone in your organization who is involved in the supervision of accounting personnel and (2) by providing copies or summaries of training materials used by your organization to improve employee communications skills. These materials will provide useful guidance for improving current educational practices.

Responses to the questionnaire will not be identified by individual or organization name. An address label is used only for the purpose of identifying nonrespondents. If you do not wish to respond, please return the blank questionnaire. Otherwise a follow-up letter will be forthcoming in about two weeks.

Copyrights and organizational policies will be observed with respect to any materials provided. These materials will not be used, quoted, or copied in any form without the written permission of your organization.

Please feel free to comment on the questionnaire or provide additional remarks which might be helpful in the project. If you wish to receive a copy of the survey results, please mark the appropriate space on the last page of the questionnaire. Direct all correspondence to:

> Dr. Robert W. Ingram
> College of Business Administration
> University of South Carolina
> Columbia, South Carolina 29208

Your assistance is appreciated.

Appendix B

Letter to Academicians

The American Accounting Association is sponsoring a research project to determine the importance of communications skills for staff accounting personnel and to evaluate the emphasis placed on developing these skills in the accounting curriculum. This research may be instrumental in identifying specific areas which warrant attention in developing accounting programs which are responsive to the needs of the accounting profession.

As part of this project, the assistance of accounting program administrators is being solicited. I would appreciate your reading the enclosed questionnaire and completing it yourself or forwarding it to the individual on your accounting faculty who is most involved in the communications skills area (perhaps the person who teaches a communications course, if one is offered).

Responses to the questionnaire will not be identified by individual or organization name. An address label is used only for the purpose of identifying nonrespondents. If you do not wish to respond, please return the blank questionnaire. Otherwise a follow-up letter will be forthcoming in about two weeks.

Please feel free to comment on the questionnaire or provide additional remarks which might be helpful in the project. Direct all correspondence to:

Dr. Robert W. Ingram
College of Business Administration
University of South Carolina
Columbia, South Carolina 39208

Your assistance is appreciated.

Appendix C

Practitioners' Questionnaire

PART I.

Listed below are a series of communications skills which may be needed by staff accounting personnel. For each of the items listed, please indicate your agreement with the following statement: (1) This is a skill frequently necessary for the successful completion of staff accountant responsibilities. Also for each item, please indicate your agreement with the statement: (2) This is a skill successfully demonstrated by most staff accountants. Please use the following scale to indicate your response:

1	2	3	4	5	6
Strongly Disagree	Disagree	Neutral	Agree	Strongly Agree	Can't Evaluate

Forms of Communication	(1) Necessary Skills	(2) Demonstrated Skills
1. Correspondence writing	1 2 3 4 5 6	1 2 3 4 5 6
2. Memorandums & informal report writing	1 2 3 4 5 6	1 2 3 4 5 6
3. Formal report writing	1 2 3 4 5 6	1 2 3 4 5 6
4. Reading speed	1 2 3 4 5 6	1 2 3 4 5 6
5. Reading comprehension	1 2 3 4 5 6	1 2 3 4 5 6
6. Informal oral presentation	1 2 3 4 5 6	1 2 3 4 5 6
7. Formal oral presentation	1 2 3 4 5 6	1 2 3 4 5 6
8. Listening attentiveness	1 2 3 4 5 6	1 2 3 4 5 6
9. Listening responsiveness	1 2 3 4 5 6	1 2 3 4 5 6
Mechanical Skills		
10. Correct grammar	1 2 3 4 5 6	1 2 3 4 5 6
11. Correct punctuation	1 2 3 4 5 6	1 2 3 4 5 6
12. Correct spelling	1 2 3 4 5 6	1 2 3 4 5 6
Logic & Organization Skills		
13. Outline development	1 2 3 4 5 6	1 2 3 4 5 6
14. Inductive reasoning	1 2 3 4 5 6	1 2 3 4 5 6
15. Deductive reasoning	1 2 3 4 5 6	
Stylistic Skills		
16. Coherence in verbal presentation	1 2 3 4 5 6	1 2 3 4 5 6
17. Clarity in verbal presentation	1 2 3 4 5 6	1 2 3 4 5 6
18. Conciseness in verbal presentation	1 2 3 4 5 6	1 2 3 4 5 6
19. Paragraph development	1 2 3 4 5 6	1 2 3 4 5 6
20. Use of visual aids	1 2 3 4 5 6	1 2 3 4 5 6

PART II.

Please indicate your assessment of the frequency of occasions in which apparent lack of communications skills is a reason for not hiring an individual for a staff accounting position. Use the following code to identify your response, and circle the appropriate number for each item:

1) Very frequently   2) Frequently   3) Sometimes
4) Not often   5) Never   6) Can't evaluate

    1. Lack of communication skills   1 2 3 4 5 6
       is primary reason

    2. Lack of communication skills   1 2 3 4 5 6
       is contributing reason

Deficiencies in which communications skills contribute most frequently to decisions not to hire an individual? (You may use item numbers from the communications skills inventory.)

Please indicate your assessment of the frequency of occasions in which apparent lack of communications skills is a reason for dismissing an individual from a staff accounting position. Use the following code to identify your response, and circle the appropriate number for each item:

1) Very frequently   2) Frequently   3) Sometimes
4) Not often   5) Never   6) Can't evaluate

    1. Lack of communication skills   1 2 3 4 5 6
       is primary reason

    2. Lack of communication skills   1 2 3 4 5 6
       is contributing reason

Deficiencies in which communciations skills contribute most frequently to decisions to dismiss an individual? (You may use item numbers from the communications skills inventory.)

PART III.

Please indicate your opinion as to whether the communications skills demonstrated by staff accounting personnel are changing over time by checking the appropriate response:

Increasing   _____
Decreasing   _____
Remaining unchanged   _____
Can't evaluate   _____

PART IV.

Does your organization have a formal program to improve employee communications skills?

Yes   _____
No   _____
Sure   _____

Do you wish to receive a copy of the questionnaire results?

Yes   _____
No   _____

Thank you for your assistance.

Appendix D

Academicians' Questionnaire

PART I.

Listed below are a series of communications skills which may be needed by staff accounting personnel. For each of the items listed, please indicate your agreement with the following statement: (1) This is a skill frequently necessary for the successful completion of staff accountant responsibilities. Also for each item, please indicate your agreement with the statement: (2) This is a skill successfully demonstrated by most accounting graduates. Please use the following scale to indicate your response:

1	2	3	4	5	6
Strongly Disagree	Disagree	Neutral	Agree	Strongly Agree	Can't Evaluate

Forms of Communication	(1) Necessary Skills	(2) Demonstrated Skills
1. Correspondence writing	1 2 3 4 5 6	1 2 3 4 5 6
2. Memorandums & informal report writing	1 2 3 4 5 6	1 2 3 4 5 6
3. Formal report writing	1 2 3 4 5 6	1 2 3 4 5 6
4. Reading speed	1 2 3 4 5 6	1 2 3 4 5 6
5. Reading comprehension	1 2 3 4 5 6	1 2 3 4 5 6
6. Informal oral presentation	1 2 3 4 5 6	1 2 3 4 5 6
7. Formal oral presentation	1 2 3 4 5 6	1 2 3 4 5 6
8. Listening attentiveness	1 2 3 4 5 6	1 2 3 4 5 6
9. Listening responsiveness	1 2 3 4 5 6	1 2 3 4 5 6
Mechanical Skills		
10. Correct grammar	1 2 3 4 5 6	1 2 3 4 5 6
11. Correct punctuation	1 2 3 4 5 6	1 2 3 4 5 6
12. Correct spelling	1 2 3 4 5 6	1 2 3 4 5 6
Logic & Organization Skills		
13. Outline development	1 2 3 4 5 6	1 2 3 4 5 6
14. Inductive reasoning	1 2 3 4 5 6	1 2 3 4 5 6
15. Deductive reasoning	1 2 3 4 5 6	
Stylistic Skills		
16. Coherence in verbal presentation	1 2 3 4 5 6	1 2 3 4 5 6
17. Clarity in verbal presentation	1 2 3 4 5 6	1 2 3 4 5 6
18. Conciseness in verbal presentation	1 2 3 4 5 6	1 2 3 4 5 6
19. Paragraph development	1 2 3 4 5 6	1 2 3 4 5 6
20. Use of visual aids	1 2 3 4 5 6	1 2 3 4 5 6

If courses in communications (other than freshman/sophomore general education requirements and advanced courses designed primarily for English and mass communications majors) are available to accounting majors plese complete Part II. Otherwise, please begin with Part III.

PART II.

1. If courses are offered at the undergraduate level please check the appropriate characteristics.

   a. communications courses are recommended
      to accounting majors   _____
   b. communications courses are required of
      accounting majors   _____
   c. communications courses are taught by
      accounting faculty   _____
   d. communications courses are taught by
      business (nonaccounting) faculty   _____
   e. communications courses are taught by
      nonbusiness faculty   _____
   f. the amount of credit offered for these
      courses is _____ (sem./quarter) hours.

2. If courses are offered at the master's level please check the appropriate characteristics.

   a. communications courses are recommended
      to accounting majors   _____
   b. communications courses are required of
      accounting majors   _____
   c. communications courses are taught by
      accounting faculty   _____
   d. communications courses are taught by
      business (nonaccounting) faculty   _____
   e. communications courses are taught by
      nonbusiness faculty   _____
   f. the amount of credit offered for these
      courses is _____ (sem./quater) hours.

If available, please provide a copy of course outlines, assignment sheets, and the titles of text materials.

PART III.

If no courses in communications skills are offered, please check the appropriate reasons.

a. inadequate marginal benefits   _____
b. lack of faculty interest   _____
c. lack of student interest   _____
d. inadequate resources   _____
e. insufficient time in program   _____
f. better alternatives   _____
    Specify:

PART IV.

1. Of the total instructional hours taken by accounting students in your program (above freshman/sophomore general education requirements) approximately what percentage are devoted primarily to the development of communications skills:

        undergraduate level   _____
        graduate level   _____

2. On average, do you believe the communications skills of your accounting graduates to be:

        Very good   _____
        Good   _____
        Satisfactory   _____
        Poor   _____
        Very poor   _____
        Can't evaluate   _____

3. Do you perceive the emphasis on developing communications skills in your program as:

        Increasing   _____
        Decreasing   _____
        Remaining unchanged   _____

4. Please indicate which degrees are offered in your program to accounting majors:

Undergraduate	_____
Masters	_____
Doctorate	_____

Do you wish to receive a copy of the survey results? Yes_____ No_____

Thank you for your assistance.

Appendix E

Definitions

The following definitions pertain to the enclosed questionnaire:

Staff Accountant - We are concerned particularly with junior level accounting personnel in the first three years of employment whose duties require active involvement in communications processes. Personnel involved in purely clerical or managerial duties are exempted from consideraion. We are using the term "staff accountant" for simplicity.

Outline - The ability to indicate systematically and schematically the main points of a given topic as well as the relationship or sequence of those points.

Inductive Reasoning - The ability to analyze a specific body of data and to generate a general conclusion based on that data.

Deductive Reasoning - The ability to reason from a general premise to specific conclusions or to apply a generalized concept to specific information.

Coherence - The ability to arrange ideas and units of information into clear, ordered, effective patterns.

Clarity - The use of precise diction and sentence structure appropriate to the information being communicated. Clarity further involves the ability to define terms unfamiliar to the reader or audience and to provide examples that help the reader understand the material being presented.

Conciseness - The use not simply of short sentences, but of direct, economical, accurate statements free of unnecessary wordiness.

Paragraph Development - The ability to arrange and relate the sentences of a paragraph in such a way that their relationship and sequence is clear to the reader and so that they arrive at a conclusion or present a unified body of information; for example, typical patterns of paragraph structure are cause-effect, comparison-contrast, classification, chronological order, etc.

SELECTED BIBLIOGRAPHY

American Institute of Certified Public Accountants. *Accounting Firms and Practitioners.* New York: AICPA, 1977.

Andrews, Deborah C. "An Interesting Course in Technical Communications." *Technical Communication* 25 (1976), pp. 12-15.

_____. *Technical Writing: Principles and Forms.* New York: MacMillan, 1978.

Andrews, J. Douglas and Robert J. Koester. "Communication Difficulties as Perceived by the Accounting Profession and Professors of Accounting." *The Journal of Business Communication* 16 (Winter 1979), pp. 33-42.

Baker, William H. and Nadine T. Ashby. "Teaching Business Writing by the Spiral Method." *The Journal of Business Communication* 14 (Spring 1977), pp. 13-21.

Bennett, James C. "The Communication Needs of Business Executives." *The Journal of Business Communication* 8 (Spring 1971), pp. 3-11.

Bromage, Mary C. "A Matter of Wording." *The Journal of Accountancy* (January 1963), pp. 59-62.

_____. "Sentences that Make Sense." *The Journal of Accountancy* (May 1967), pp. 56-60.

_____. "Wording the Management Audit Report." *The Journal of Accountancy* (February 1972), pp. 50-57.

Burger, Robert S. "How to Write So People Can Better Understand You." *The Journal of Accountancy* (July 1974), pp. 84-88.

Clark, Robert B. "How Relevant is Accounting Education?" *The Journal of Accountancy* (February 1973), pp. 90-91.

"Comparison of Communication Curricular Patterns and Objectives with Communication Needs of Business." *ABCA Bulletin* 36 (June 1973), pp. 11-13.

Cox, Homer L. "Opinions of Selected Business Managers About Some Aspects of Communication on the Job." *The Journal of Business Communication* 6 (Fall 1968), pp. 3-12.

DeBeaugrande, Robert. "Information and Grammar in Technical Writing." *College Composition and Communication* 28 (December 1977), pp. 235-332.

Foley, Louis. "Brevity Isn't Everything." *The Journal of Business Communication* 12 (Fall 1974), pp. 30-34.

Grogg, William. "The Importance of Business Writing to the Student — A Businessman's Viewpoint." *ABCA Bulletin* 35 (June 1972), pp. 1-5.

Grove, Hugh D. and Richard S. Savich. "Attitude Research in Accounting: A Model for Reliability and Validity Considerations." *The Accounting Review* (July 1979), pp. 522-527.

Hart, Sara. "Key Philosophical Factors in Developing a Business Communication Curriculum." *The Journal of Business Communication* 13 (Summer 1976), pp. 47-57.

Hasselback, James R. *Accounting Faculty 1977-1978*. College Station, Texas: Aviso Publications, 1977.

"How Undergraduate Business Communication Programs Can Meet the Communication Needs of Business." *ABCA Bulletin* 36 (June 1973), pp. 14-17.

Huegli, Jon M. and Harvey D. Tschirgi. "an Investigation of Communication Skills Application and Effectiveness at the Entry Job Level." *The Journal of Business Communication* 12 (Fall 1974), pp. 24-29.

James, Don L. and Ronald L. Decker. "Does Business Student Preparation Satisfy Personnel Officers?" *Collegiate News and Views* 27 (Spring 1974), pp. 26-30.

John, Richard C. "Improve Your Technical Writing." *Management Accounting* (September 1976), pp. 49-52.

Knapper, Arno F. "Good Writing — A Shared Responsibility." *The Journal of Business Communication* 15 (Winter 1978), pp. 23-27.

Larsen, E. John. "Thoughts on Writing." *The Journal of Accountancy* (September 1973), pp. 102-103.

Larson, Richard L. "English: An Enabling Discipline." *ADE Bulletin* 46 (September 1975), pp. 3-7.

Lewis, Phillip. "Communication Competency and Collegiate Schools of Business." *College News and Views* (Winter 1975-76), pp. 35-45.

Ley, Patricia S. "Style in Analytical Writing." *The Journal of Commercial Bank Lending* (April 1974), pp. 61-66.

Locker, Kitty. "Patterns of Organization for Business Writing." *Journal of Business Communication* 14 (Spring 1977), pp. 35-45.

MacIntosh, Fred H. "Teaching Writing for the World's Work." *The Teaching of Technical Writing*. Urbana, Illinois: National Council of Teachers of English, 1975.

Marder, Daniel. *The Craft of Technical Writing*. Iowa: Kendall Hunt Publishing Co., 1978.

Mathes, J.C. and Dwight Stevenson. *Designing Technical Reports*. Indianapolis, Indiana: Bobbs-Merrill, 1976.

Oppenheim, A.N. *Questionnaire Design and Attitude Measurement*. New York: Basic Books, 1966.

Penrose, John M. "A Survey of the Perceived Importance of Business Communication Education." *The Journal of Business Communication* 13 (Winter 1976), pp. 17-24.

Rainey, Bill G. "Professors and Executives Appraise Business Communication Education." *The Journal of Business Communication* 9 (Summer 1972), pp. 19-23.

Rice, Joseph A. "Johnny, The Grad You Hired Last Week, Can't Write." *Supervisory Management* (September 1976), pp. 14-21.

Roy, Robert H. and James H. MacNeill. "Written and Spoken English for the Accountant." *The Journal of Business Communication* 7 (Summer 1970), pp. 39-44.

Sigband, Norman B. "Communication for Results." *Governmental Finance* (February 1977), pp. 10-14.

Sparrow, W. Keats. "Six Myths About Writing for Business and Industry." *The Technical Writing Teacher* 3 (Winter 1976), pp. 49-59.

Stine, Donna and Donald Skarzenski. "Priorities for the Business Communication Classroom: A Survey of Business and Academe." *The Journal of Business Communication* 16 (Spring 1979), pp. 15-30.

Struck, H.R. "Wanted: More Writing Courses for Graduate Students." *College Composition and Communication* (May 1971), p. 192.

Strunk, William and E.B. White. *The Elements of Style.* New York: MacMillan, 1959.

Sullivan, Jerimiah J. "The Importance of a Philosophical 'Mix' in Teaching Business Communication." *The Journal of Business Communication* 15 (Summer 1978), pp. 29-37.

Swenson, Lloyd A. "A More Meaningful Business Communications Class." *The Balance Sheet* (May 1973), pp. 359, 380.

Swift, Marvin H. "Clear Writing Means Clear Thinking . . ." *Harvard Business Review* (January-February 1973), pp. 59-62.

"Views of Business Representatives About Communication Needs of Business." *ABCA Bulletin* 36 (June 1973), pp. 4-11.

Weeks, Francis W. "Current Issues in the Practice of Business Communication in the U.S.A." *Journal of Business Communication* 13 (Spring 1976), pp. 61-68.

White, Myron L. "How Badly Does Management Want Good Business Writing?" *The Journal of Business Communication* 3 (March 1966), pp. 15-26.